Redbird Relics

Treasures from the St. Louis Cardinals Museum

A chronological journey through the rich history of the St. Louis Cardinals featuring artifacts from the museum collection.

Written by Brian Finch

Design and graphics by Gary Kodner

Photography by Dan Donovan

Edited by Jeff Scott

Contributors

Brian Finch, Author

Brian is responsible for the museum's writing and research, visitor services and educational programming as the Manager of Stadium Tours and Museum Outreach. He is a lifelong Cardinals fan originally from Hopkinsville, Ky. and joined the team in 2004.

Gary Kodner, Creative Director

Gary has worked with the Cardinals for over 30 years through Busch Creative Services and his own company, Nehmen-Kodner Creative Services. He has enjoyed working on a number of logo and signage projects for the club, putting to use his lifelong fandom of the team.

Dan Donovan, Photographer

Dan covers the Cardinals through his lens as a commercial photographer, shooting both action and feature photos for the franchise. His work has provided a rich visual history of the club for over 30 years.

Jeff Scott, Editor

Jeff is a freelance writer who enjoys baseball research and memorabilia forensics. He authored most of the copy accompanying displays throughout the Cardinals Museum and has contributed to the Cardinals Yearbook.

This book would not have been possible without significant contributions from the following Cardinals team members:

Museum Curatorial Staff

Paula Homan – Curator
Amy Berra – Assistant Curator
Sarah Rybicki – Registrar

Front Office Staff

Vicki Bryant – Vice President, Event Services
  & Merchandising
Nate Green – Director, Cardinals Nation
Ron Watermon – Vice President, Communications
Taka Yanagimoto – Manager, Photography
Steve Zesch – Director, Publications

Thanks also to Dan Farrell, Mike Whittle, Brad Wood, Joe Strohm, Jim Gilstrap, Gabe Kiley, Tom Klein, Stan McNeal, Julie Laningham, Grace Kell, John Lowry, Kelly Cheatham, Molly Becker, Rob Fasoldt, Jennifer Needham, Kerry Emerson, Martin Coco, Kathy Langenfeld, Melissa Tull, Chris Molina, Kristen Schmalz, Greg Pauli, Ashley Brown, Jennifer Johnston and Debra Dennler.

First Printing

Printed in the United States of America by NIES, an RR Donnelley Company

ISBN: 978-0-692-54883-7

Library of Congress: 2015917393

Copyright © 2015 St. Louis Cardinals, LLC • Published by St. Louis Cardinals Hall of Fame & Museum • 601 Clark Street, St. Louis, MO 63102

Contents

Contents

Baseball Like it Oughta Be

ne Run Chase
of 1998

100 TH
ANNIVERSARY
1892 1992

Cardinals
9

Cardinals
47

HOLDING HISTORY

HOLDING
HISTORY

HOLDING
HISTORY
RULES

HOLDING
HISTORY

Whitey Ball

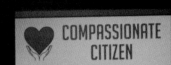

COMPASSIONATE
CITIZEN

Civic Center
Busch Memorial
Stadium Model

1966 - 2005

Foreword by Bill DeWitt Jr. and Bill DeWitt III

The Cardinals are one of the most storied franchises in baseball with a remarkably rich history that spans more than 125 years in St. Louis.

We feel very fortunate that our family has played a small part in that history.

Bill DeWitt Sr.'s 60-plus year career in baseball began in 1916 when he started selling soda at Robison Field baseball games. He joined the Cardinals front office as a protégé of Branch Rickey, and under Mr. Rickey's mentorship, he learned about baseball and the business behind it. He would later move to the St. Louis Browns to become general manager and, eventually, the owner. After 35-plus years with the Cardinals and Browns, he moved on to general manager and/or ownership roles with the Yankees, Tigers, Reds and White Sox. But, it all started in St. Louis, so it was particularly special for us to have the opportunity to join the Cardinals in 1996.

We were initially very impressed with the team's museum collection, which was ahead of its time. The best items in the collection were from the legendary career of Stan Musial, who donated a significant portion of his personal memorabilia so his countless fans could enjoy them. But, we also noticed that there were significant gaps in the collection. For whatever reason, professional sports teams never used to prioritize the preservation of their history by collecting artifacts along the way. So, we decided that we would attempt to acquire important Cardinals artifacts in a variety of different ways.

We started by participating in sports memorabilia auctions, many of which would have Cardinals items featured along with other teams rich in baseball history. Cardinals fans have been great collectors over the years—don't we all know someone with a basement full of bobbleheads, jerseys and ticket stubs? Then, in 1998 and 1999, legendary collector Barry Halper put his personal collection up for private sale and auction. His was no ordinary collection — when the auctioneer slammed the final hammer, the proceeds approached $30 million. Fortunately, we were able to acquire Branch Rickey's 1919 manager's uniform and one of Dizzy Dean's jerseys from 1936-37, relics of two legendary contributors to the franchise. Other significant purchases have included Bob Gibson's 1968 Cy Young Award, Grover Cleveland Alexander's 1926 road jersey and Lou Brock's 3,000th-hit bat, to name a few.

Next, we reached out to or were approached by private collectors directly when the word got out that we were interested in purchasing Cardinals items of significance. We were often glad to hear comments from collectors such as, "I would never sell this item to anyone but the Cardinals, because I trust you will display it for the fans." A good example of this was our transaction with local antique rug dealer Nick Bendas, who had assembled the best collection of vintage Cardinals jerseys anywhere. Not only did he have several historically significant early jerseys, but he also had researched them in great detail and was helpful in passing along his knowledge of Cardinals uniforms to our museum staff.

And finally, we began making it a priority to approach our players or fans directly when they were involved in great moments. For example, we received Yadier Molina's game-

Foreword

winning home run bat from Game 7 of the 2006 National League Championship Series. He was actually thrilled that we asked! Mike Matheny generously donated the glove he used to set the National League errorless streak as a catcher. And who can forget David Freese's performance in the 2011 World Series? After getting "shredded" at home plate following his walk-off, Game 6 home run, David ended up with one "half" of his jersey and promptly gave it to a representative of Cooperstown who approached him in the locker room. The other half was tossed into the arms of a young fan in the front row. After making a small donation to the girl's college fund to get it back, we were thrilled to have such a memorable item to tell the story of that remarkable World Series. Over the years, our outstanding Museum team, led by curator Paula Homan and history buff Brian Finch,

From left to right, Bill De Witt Jr., Bob Gibson, Ozzie Smith, Red Schoendienst, Whitey Herzog, Lou Brock, Tony La Russa, Bill DeWitt III, on April 7, 2014, the Museum's grand opening.

spent many hours helping us research, collect, authenticate, preserve and display our growing collection of Redbird Relics. Today, the Cardinals collection is the largest of any team in Major League Baseball and is second only to the National Baseball Hall of Fame in Cooperstown in terms of its size.

In 2014, we were able to realize our dream of opening a world-class Museum and Hall of Fame inside Cardinals Nation at Ballpark Village to share this amazing collection with our fans, and to honor the greatest contributors to the franchise over the years. With great artifacts, interactive exhibits and rotating galleries, it is a place fans can visit frequently and learn something new every time.

This book is an effort to celebrate the great artifacts and memorabilia from the Museum with beautiful photographs and descriptions of the items on display. But, it is also an educational book with well-researched essays that illuminate the artifacts and relive some of the greatest moments, milestones and people who helped create the amazing story of the St. Louis Cardinals.

We hope you marvel at the artifacts and enjoy the stories behind them, tales that remind us how baseball can bind the generations together in St. Louis. We also hope you make a pilgrimage to Ballpark Village to visit our Museum and see these items in person. In the meantime, we will do our best to field great teams that continue to create memories — and artifacts — for future generations to enjoy.

– by Bill DeWitt Jr., Principal Owner & CEO, and Bill DeWitt III, President

The 1944 "Street Car Series" exhibit in the Sportsman's Park Gallery at the Cardinals Hall of Fame and Museum.

Introduction

Interest in sports was at an all-time high in St. Louis in 1966 after the opening of Civic Center Busch Memorial Stadium, a new downtown, multipurpose venue that would play host to the city's professional baseball and football teams. Just blocks away, the Hawks were still hosting National Basketball Association contests. And about a month before the Cardinals christened their new ballpark, it was announced that a National Hockey League team would soon be coming to town.

Fans enjoying the original St. Louis Sports Hall of Fame in Busch Memorial Stadium.

In response to the fans' support, and purportedly at the request of Cardinals President August A. Busch Jr., an idea was hatched to honor the best St. Louis athletes in a specially designed space inside the new stadium. The St. Louis Sports Hall of Fame was launched and officially opened its doors June 20, 1968.

The Civic Center Redevelopment Corporation, owners of the stadium, enlisted the help of an advisory board that included, among others, legendary sportswriters Bob Broeg and Bob Burnes; former Cardinals shortstop Marty Marion; C.C. Johnson Spink, publisher of *The Sporting News*; and Bob Hyland, general manager of KMOX Radio. This group developed displays of memorabilia with assistance from organizations in the community that featured baseball, football, hockey, golf, bowling, soccer and tennis.

The original museum was allocated about 10,000 square feet of space on the lower level of Busch Stadium, below the main souvenir shop. Exhibits on basketball, boxing and Olympic achievements specific to St. Louis athletes were added, as was a Broadcasters and Sportswriters Hall of Fame that featured notable media personalities from the turn-of-

the-century to the recent past.

The space was renovated and transformed over the years to keep pace with changing times, but stayed true to its purpose of honoring athletes who brought fame and glory to the city of St. Louis — whether they played here as professionals, or were raised here and had taken their talents elsewhere.

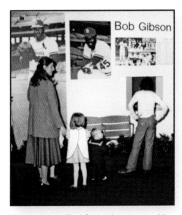

The facility profiled St. Louis sports and its professional stars.

The ballpark was sold to the Cardinals in 1984, but the Civic Center Corporation (successor to the Civic Center Redevelopment Corporation) maintained ownership of the Hall of Fame and initiated a renovation that reduced the total square footage of the facility.

The next major overhaul would change the entire scope of the operation. In preparation for the Cardinals' 100th anniversary in 1992, the team worked with the Hall of Fame to create an exhibit looking back at the history of the franchise.

In 1992, the newly remodeled Cardinals Hall of Fame Museum opened with an exhibit celebrating the club's 100 years in the National League.

Introduction

Stan Musial, the greatest player to wear the birds on the bat, was asked if he would consider donating memorabilia from his illustrious career. Just as he had done 475 times in his big league career, "The Man" knocked it out of the park. Musial ultimately donated more than 1,300 items, and the new St. Louis Cardinals Hall of Fame Museum opened its doors Feb. 3, 1992, kicking off centennial celebration events that would span the entire season.

The newly designed museum provided a chronological look at the club's history from 1892 through 1992. The Musial Room became a focal point, highlighting "The Man's" achievements on and off the field. Other sections covered late-19th century history, St. Louis Negro League teams and the American League St. Louis Browns.

In 1996, the brewery sold the ballclub, stadium and museum to a group led by Bill DeWitt Jr. The St. Louis baseball lineage in DeWitt's family ran deep; his father was the secretary and treasurer of the Cardinals during the Gas House Gang years under Branch Rickey, and was owner and general manager of the Browns in the 1940s and early 1950s. In 1997, the new

Mark McGwire's 1962 Cardinal-red Corvette, on display at the Cardinals Hall of Fame Museum from 2000 through 2008.

owners moved the Cardinals Hall of Fame Museum out of Busch Stadium and across the street into the International Bowling Hall of Fame's building.

Guests were able to enjoy two sports museums for one admission price. In the Cardinals area, fans could explore the vintage game or the modern game, as laid out on each side of the museum. Following the historic home run chase of 1998, visitors could see Mark McGwire's 1962 Cardinal-red Corvette on display, which the club had given him after he hit home run No. 62.

Busch Stadium III opened in 2006 with plans for Ballpark Village to be built on the site of the previous stadium. While Museum staffers prepared to close their existing gallery and locate to the new one, the International Bowling Museum and Hall of Fame accepted an invitation to join two other bowling industry groups on a campus in Arlington, Texas, and moved its operations there.

The Cardinals formally broke ground on Ballpark Village on a frigid February day in 2013, announcing it would be ready

The Museum's grand entrance in the International Bowling Museum, which highlighted the team's World Series championship trophies.

Introduction

in time for Opening Day 2014. The club turned to the award-winning design firm PGAV for the museum attraction, but added a new twist. While the facility's name had always been

Each stadium gallery in the Museum features a ballpark model with video highlights from that era in Cardinals history.

the St. Louis Cardinals Hall of Fame Museum, the club had never had its own, true Hall of Fame—it had simply honored those players with a connection to the Cardinals who were already enshrined in Cooperstown. The new institution would be the St. Louis Cardinals Hall of Fame *and* Museum, with plans that included a plaque gallery for the members deemed worthy of the Cardinals red jacket.

The facility opened to great fanfare April 7, 2014. Along with the Museum, the Cardinals Hall of Fame presented by Edward Jones was dedicated with 22 inaugural members. Honorees included players who were already in the National Baseball Hall of Fame specifically as Cardinals, along with those who had had their numbers retired by the organization. Later that

season, the team inducted its first class of Hall of Famers in what would be the start of an annual tradition.

The new Museum includes seven galleries housed in 8,000 square feet of space on the second level of Cardinals Nation. The Championship Gallery, containing all of the team's World Series trophies and rings, pays tribute to each year the club won the ultimate prize. The interactive exhibits use modern technology to spark the interest of fans of all ages, and the Holding History exhibit, where visitors put on gloves and hold game-used bats and World Series rings, gets fans as close as possible to the historical artifacts.

The collection itself includes more than 22,000 items and 80,000 vintage photographs. It's considered the largest single-team-focused collection in professional sports. The artifacts on the following pages represent the "best of the best," spanning Hall of Fame players, milestone moments and championship victories. The title speaks for itself—*Redbird Relics: Treasures from the St. Louis Cardinals Museum.*

The club dedicated its Hall of Fame on Opening Day in 2014 with 22 inaugural members and holds an annual ceremony for new inductees.

A framed Ladies Day promotional silk from 1887; a scorebook from the Browns' last season in the American Association in 1891; the cover of Von der Ahe's personal rule book; and his baseball card from the 1887 Old Judge set.

Chris Von der Ahe

More than seven decades before Anheuser-Busch bought the Cardinals franchise — a savvy move that helped the brewery's sales skyrocket — a similarly motivated saloon owner named Chris Von der Ahe acquired the defunct St. Louis Brown Stockings in hopes it would boost his bottom line.

Von der Ahe, a German immigrant who moved to St. Louis in 1870, ran a grocery store and bar just one block away from the Grand Avenue Grounds, where baseball games involving the St. Louis Brown Stockings were among the venue's most popular draws. Von der Ahe knew very little about baseball, but he clearly understood the nearby contests were responsible for his saloon being busy before and after games — and nearly empty while games were in progress.

The Brown Stockings folded before the 1878 season because of a game-fixing scandal, and Von der Ahe's saloon suffered as a result. Ned Cuthbert, a former leftfielder for the Brown Stockings and one of Von der Ahe's bartenders, reminded his boss that large crowds paid to attend baseball games and typically enjoyed a drink or two while at the ballpark. If Von der Ahe owned a team, not only would his establishment benefit from pre- and postgame crowds, but he also would have a monopoly on concessions at the park. The concept appealed to the ambitious and colorful Von der Ahe, and by 1880, he was the proud owner of the former Brown Stockings franchise.

After a year of matching up against semipro opponents and any foe that would draw a crowd, Von der Ahe joined businessmen from five other cities in late 1881 to establish the American Association. The upstart major league would capitalize on two of the National League's perceived shortcomings; the NL didn't schedule games on Sundays and prohibited alcohol sales at the ballpark. American Association games quickly found an audience and Von der Ahe became a wealthy man.

Revenue generated by games and other business ventures emboldened Von der Ahe to pour money into his team, known simply as the Browns by 1883, and solicit the best players around. His audacity helped the ballclub achieve unprecedented success; the Browns won four straight league championships from 1885 through 1888.

Aggressive expansion, though, left the league on shaky ground. Seeking stability, the American Association merged with the more-established National League in 1892. Von der Ahe continued as the Browns' owner, but a string of personal and business failures left him in a tenuous financial position. The final blow came in 1898 when the club's grandstand burned to the ground. Facing a tailspin of legal troubles and debt, Von der Ahe was forced to sell the club.

The franchise was purchased at auction in March 1899 by a representative of Von der Ahe's creditors and flipped almost immediately to an agent for brothers Frank and Stanley Robison. Von der Ahe returned to bartending and, by 1908, the former millionaire claimed assets of only $200. Though his legacy had been tarnished, Von der Ahe will forever be hailed as the man who single-handedly brought professional baseball to prominence in St. Louis.

"Chris Von der Ahe did as much for baseball in St. Louis and the country at large as any man ever associated with the game."
– Al Spink, founder of *The Sporting News*

Pitcher Bill Sherdel and Cardinals Manager Branch Rickey (right).

Branch Rickey's 1919 road jersey from his first season in the dugout as Cardinals manager.

Branch Rickey

The greatest innovator baseball has ever known nearly missed his calling as a front-office executive because of his preference for being in the dugout.

A few years after his short and unremarkable career as a major league catcher ended, Branch Rickey accepted a scouting position with the St. Louis Browns and soon found himself promoted to field manager. As Browns skipper, he was obsessed with strategy and theory, and became fascinated with statistical analysis and developing new ways to teach and train players. Rickey later invented, popularized or endorsed the batting tee, sliding pit, pitching machine and an early form of radar.

Rickey's scholarly approach to the game and refusal to manage on Sundays didn't sit well with new Browns owner, Phil Ball, who demoted Rickey back to scout after the 1915 season. Cardinals leadership, which had been observing Rickey and became enamored with him, offered the disgruntled Rickey the position of team president in 1917. He jumped at the opportunity, though his new job would have to wait as Rickey served his country during World War I.

Rickey returned in 1919 as Cardinals president and named himself manager — partly to save the financially shaky club another salary, and partly because he loved being in uniform. He donned the jersey on the opposite page during that first season in St. Louis. The heavy flannel road garment was acquired by the team in 1999, and today is the oldest jersey in the Cardinals Museum collection.

As he had done with the Browns, Rickey delivered clubhouse talks that were more scientific than energetic. His style didn't resonate with his mostly undereducated players, and the Cards never finished higher than third place. In 1925, owner Sam Breadon relieved Rickey of his dugout duties and asked him to focus his talents in the front office. A disappointed Rickey almost left the game he loved, but accepted the offer and set out to improve the team by exploiting a rule change that would revolutionize baseball.

Before 1921, major league clubs could not own minor league franchises. Minor league clubs operated independently and profited by selling their best players to major league teams. The cash-strapped Cardinals typically came up short bidding against other franchises. With the ownership rule eliminated, Rickey saw an opportunity. The Cardinals sold their ballpark — opting to rent Sportsman's Park from the rival Browns — and used the proceeds to purchase full or majority ownership in three minor league teams.

With baseball's first farm system established, the Cardinals could sign young players and let them refine their skills until they were major league ready. The results were almost immediate; the 1926 Cardinals claimed the franchise's first World Series championship with 14 players who were products of the farm system.

Casual baseball fans today recognize Rickey as the man who signed Jackie Robinson for the Brooklyn Dodgers, breaking baseball's color barrier, but Rickey's farm system model radically changed the game as well. And it all happened because Branch Rickey reluctantly agreed to trade his wool jersey for a wool suit and bowtie.

"I'm doing you the greatest favor one man ever has done to another."
– Cardinals Owner Sam Breadon, to Branch Rickey after Rickey was fired as manager and asked to move into a front-office position

Knot Hole Gang membership cards, which granted youth free access to home games.

Boy's Ticket...Season 1935
CARDINAL KNOT HOLE GANG Nᵒ 7026
James Tighe
Is a regular member of the Cardinal Knot Hole Gang, and
has subscribed to the agreement on the back of this card.
AGENCY *St. John Baptist School*
S. Breadon
President
J. Hugo Grimm
Chairman
Executive Committee
Not good Sundays or Holidays.
This Card Good for Admission
When Presented at the Gate.

Letters and No. *A13T 39*
Ticket—Cardinal Knot Hole Gang
This Ticket will not be honored unless Membership
Card with corresponding number is shown
Date ....
Agency Secretary.

1927
MEMBERSHIP CARD   Letters and No. *BO 28*
CARDINAL KNOT HOLE GANG
Joseph Vohsen
Is a regular member of the Cardinal Knot Hole Gang, and has subscribed
to the agreement on the back of this card.
Agency *Perpetual Help School*
J. Hugo Grimm   *Clarence F. Lloyd*
Chairman Executive Committee   Executive Secretary
ALWAYS TAKE THIS CARD TO THE GAME

BOY'S MEMBERSHIP CARD
1939 — BASEBALL'S 100th ANNIVERSARY — 1939
Cardinal Knot Hole Gang
Thomas D. Mahoney
Is a regular member of the Cardinal Knot Hole Gang, and
has subscribed to the agreement on the back of this card.
AGENCY ....
J. Hugo Grimm, Chr. Exec. Comm.
Arthur Fetzner, Secretary
Nᵒ 4807
Not Good on Sundays or Holidays
Present Card at Gate for Admission.
S. Breadon
President

BOY'S TICKET—SEASON 1934
CARDINAL KNOT HOLE GANG   Nᵒ 27206
Joe Medwick
Thomas D. Mahoney
Is a regular member of the Cardinal Knot Hole Gang, and has
subscribed to the agreement on the back of this card.
Agency *U. S. Coudy » 139 Merchants Exchange*
J. Hugo Grimm   *S. Breadon*
Chairman Executive Committee   President
Not good Saturdays, Sundays or Holidays
This Card Good for Admission When Presented at the Gate

AGREEMENT OF MEMBERSHIP in the
CARDINAL KNOT HOLE GANG
In becoming a member of the Cardinal Knot Hole Gang, and in
accepting ticket to the games of the Cardinals, I agree that—
1. I will not at any time miss school to attend a game.
2. I will attend no game against the wishes of my parents or employer.
3. I will uphold the principles of clean speech, clean sports and clean
habits, and will stand with the rest of the Gang against cigarettes and
profane language on the field.
4. I will not give this card or lend it to another boy.
I understand that a breaking of this agreement may cost me my
membership in the Cardinal Knot Hole Gang.
Robert Judson
35   · Boy Must Sign Here.

The Knot Hole Gang

With the looming threat of a new ownership group moving the Cardinals out of St. Louis, a civic-minded leader stepped in and created a plan to raise capital to purchase the club — and provide a way for the city's youth to attend and enjoy professional baseball.

In 1917, team owner Helene Hathaway Britton — the first female owner of a major professional sports franchise — decided to sell the club after enduring several seasons of last-place finishes and empty grandstands. Her attorney, James C. Jones, grew concerned that a certain potential buyer would move the franchise to Cincinnati, so he devised a plan to purchase the team from Britton. Since he didn't have enough capital to buy the club outright, he created incentives to attract wealthy investors. One enticement was the "Knot Hole Gang," a program that would provide season passes to underprivileged youngsters.

Some 750 fans stepped up to acquire shares of the club. Those who invested $25 or more could offer a Knot Hole Gang pass to boys in the community. What seemed like a fine idea to serve the disadvantaged children in St. Louis fell flat, however. Branch Rickey, who became team president in 1919, recognized that "the men who bought the shares knew boys with ample spending money and hardly any who needed to be taken off the streets. Because the 'overprivileged' boys, so to speak, declined the gratuitous admissions, we had no Knot Holers at all at the first half-dozen games for the first season."

Rickey convinced shareholders to turn their Knot Hole Gang passes back over to the team, which in turn, would offer them to local organizations serving youth in the community. Together with the ballclub, these groups selected boys between ages 10 and 16 to participate in the program, provided they had their parents' consent, were not skipping school to watch games and adhered to the Knot Hole Gang Code of Conduct. With the new arrangement, the program exploded with interest. By some accounts, more than 12,000 boys came to games for free during the first season.

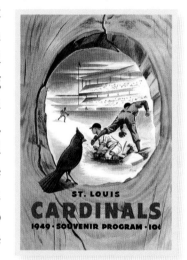

This 1949 scorecard featuring a cardinal watching the action through a knot hole in the fence harkens back to the genesis of the Knot Hole Gang.

The program would open up to girls a few years later and continue to evolve, adding rules and expectations of citizenship and sportsmanship. If St. Louis had been an evenly divided town in the early 1920s, balanced between the American League Browns and the National League Cardinals, this program — along with the Cardinals' emergence as a perennial contender — tipped the scales. Many Knot Hole Gang members and their families became loyal, lifelong Redbird supporters and helped build the foundation for the strong fan base that exists today.

> *"When they grow up into young men and women, they will continue to be fans and support the game to which they were attracted in their youth."*
> – *The Sporting News* on the Knot Hole Gang, June 11, 1931

Rogers Hornsby

Considered by many as the greatest right-handed hitter of all time, Rogers Hornsby terrorized the National League with his lumber as a member of the Cardinals from 1915 to 1926. He batted over .400 in 1922, 1924 and 1925, and captured the National League Triple Crown in 1922 and 1925, making him the only player in the history of the game to accomplish both feats on multiple occasions.

Hornsby landed on the Redbirds' radar in 1915 after a spring exhibition game with his unaffiliated minor league club, the Denison Railroaders of the Western Association. He was scouted throughout the season, offered a contract in August, and made his major league debut in September. The 19-year-old shortstop, who reportedly weighed only 135 pounds, did little to impress during his one-month stint with the sixth-place Redbirds. His .246 batting average and eight errors in 18 games was not indicative of the player he would become.

"Rajah" returned in 1916 with 25 more pounds on his frame, the result of an offseason working on his uncle's farm. His batting average jumped to .313, and his slugging percentage of .444 ranked fourth in the league. He played primarily on the left side of the infield that year, but got his first taste of second base — for two innings.

In his second full season, Hornsby led the league in triples, slugging and total bases. If OPS (on-base plus slugging percentage) and WAR (wins above replacement) were recognized statistics in 1917, he would have been hailed as the best player in the National League. After a couple mere mortal seasons, Hornsby went on an amazing six-year tear that saw him top all NL hitters in batting average, on-base percentage and slugging percentage six times; total bases five times; runs batted in, hits and doubles four times; and home runs twice. During the last year of that run, Hornsby was installed as player-manager, and the following season, he lead the Cardinals to their first world championship.

While Hornsby was considered a quiet presence in the batter's box, rarely arguing balls and strikes, he could be cantankerous and outspoken off the field. Cardinals owner Sam Breadon tolerated his antics for years, but when Hornsby demanded a $50,000 salary for three years following the 1926 championship season, he was traded to the New York Giants in exchange for Frankie Frisch and Jimmy Ring.

Hornsby returned to the Cardinals in 1933 and donned this jersey (opposite page) primarily as a pinch-hitter for manager Gabby Street. However, Hornsby requested and received his release in late July so he could sign with the St. Louis Browns and become their player-manager. To this day, Hornsby still ranks in the top 10 of every major Cardinals hitting category, and his .359 batting average while with the Redbirds remains the highest in club history.

> *"My biggest thrill in baseball was making a simple tag on a runner trying to steal second base."*
> – Rogers Hornsby, recalling his tag of Babe Ruth, who was caught stealing to end the 1926 World Series

Rogers Hornsby's 1933 game-worn home jersey from his second stint with the Cardinals, one of his bats used during his hitting dominance throughout the 1920's and an autographed baseball.

Rogers Hornsby

Jesse Haines

A year into his tenure with the club, vice president Branch Rickey knew something had to change. Since joining the National League 28 seasons earlier, the Cardinals had finished no higher than third place, and that had happened only twice. The team desperately needed talent, but in the years before Rickey could create his farm system, the only ways to acquire it were through trades or buying minor leaguers. Fortunately, Rickey had a keen eye for talent—and he had set his sights on a young pitcher who had appeared in just one game with the Cincinnati Reds in 1918.

Jesse Haines was scouted by the Cardinals in 1919 while playing in the minors for Kansas City. Rickey was so enthralled with the young pitcher that he persuaded Cardinals owner James C. Jones to borrow the $10,000 it would take to sign him. Rickey was spot-on in his assessment; Haines made an immediate impact and spent the next 18 seasons wearing the Birds on the Bat. He was the last minor league player purchased by the Cardinals before the institution of the farm system.

The Cardinals still struggled as a team upon his arrival in 1920, but Haines was precisely what they needed to begin turning things around. He tossed a career-high 302.1 innings with a sub-3.00 earned-run average, and led the league with 47 appearances in his first campaign. On July 17, 1924, he pitched the first no-hitter in franchise history and would collect 20 or more wins on three occasions. His best season came in 1927 when he won 24 games and led the National League with 25 complete games and six shutouts.

"Pop," a nickname earned later in his career because of his influence on younger pitchers, continued to play a critical role in the team's success after his move to the bullpen in the early 1930s. He is one of only three pitchers in franchise history to appear in four different World Series, and would have pitched in five Fall Classics had it not been for a late-season shoulder injury in 1931. When Haines retired following the 1937 season, he was the franchise's winningest pitcher with 210 victories. He also was the last remaining Cardinals player to have participated in the club's first World Series championship in 1926.

The Cardinals Museum collection includes a home white jersey (opposite page) donned by Haines between 1933 and 1935. While clearly showing game use, the garment remains in outstanding condition. It includes his chain-stitched name on the front — "J.J. Haines," for Jesse Joseph Haines — and number 16 on the back. This is one of the earliest shirts in the collection to feature a uniform number on the back, a practice started in 1932. It was acquired from a family in the St. Louis-metropolitan area whose father had been longtime friends with Haines and had received it as a gift from the venerable pitcher.

"When I saw how hard a nice old man like Pop could take it after losing a game, I realized why he'd been a consistent winner and the Cardinals, too. I never forgot how much Haines expected of himself and of others." – Terry Moore, Cardinals outfielder, 1935-48

Jesse Haines' home jersey worn during one season between 1933 and 1935. The club used this same style for three seasons, which included a world championship in 1934.

Jim Bottomley

The first bona fide star to emerge from Branch Rickey's burgeoning farm system came from an unlikely locale, a farming and coal mining community of about 3,500 people in central Illinois.

Jim Bottomley dropped out of Nokomis High School at age 16 to help his family make ends meet. He generated income through a series of jobs and by playing semipro baseball. Rickey signed the slugging first baseman after a tryout, and Bottomley rose quickly through the minors.

He batted .325 in 37 games his rookie season in St. Louis and earned a starting role the following year, in which he posted a .371 batting average and .425 on-base percentage—both second in the National League to teammate Rogers Hornsby. Offensive production, matching uniforms and positions on the right side of the infield were about all the two sluggers had in common. Hornsby's cold and belligerent personality made him difficult to get along with, while the soft-spoken Bottomley was known as "Sunny Jim" because of his cheerful demeanor. He constantly had a smile on his face and always wore his hat cocked a little to the side.

On Sept. 16, 1924, Bottomley set a Major League Baseball record with 12 runs batted in during a single game — a feat that stood unmatched for almost seven

decades. During the Cardinals' historic 1926 pennant chase, he led the senior circuit in runs batted in, doubles and total bases. His 10 hits and .345 batting average in the Fall Classic helped lead the Redbirds over the Yankees.

Bottomley's finest season came in 1928 when he led the league in home runs, runs batted in, triples and total bases, and was recognized as the National League's Most Valuable Player. Though he hit .348 in 1931 and just missed capturing a batting title, injuries limited Bottomley's availability during the club's world championship run. He was traded to Cincinnati following the 1932 season. He came back to St. Louis in 1936 as a member of the American League Browns and retired following the 1937 campaign.

Never one to forget his roots, "Sunny Jim" frequently returned to his hometown before and after baseball seasons to play in charity games and community contests. This jersey (opposite page), which mimics the Cardinals' 1928 uniforms made by Rawlings, was tailored for Bottomley by a competing outfit, the Sainz Athletic Company. The single bird-on-a-bat logo appeared only on certain Redbird uniforms in 1927 and 1928 before the club returned to the more familiar two-birds crest in 1929.

> "They called him 'Sunny Jim' and he was sure all of that. What a fine gentleman he was, and a great ballplayer. He could do it all."
> – Les Bell, Cardinals teammate

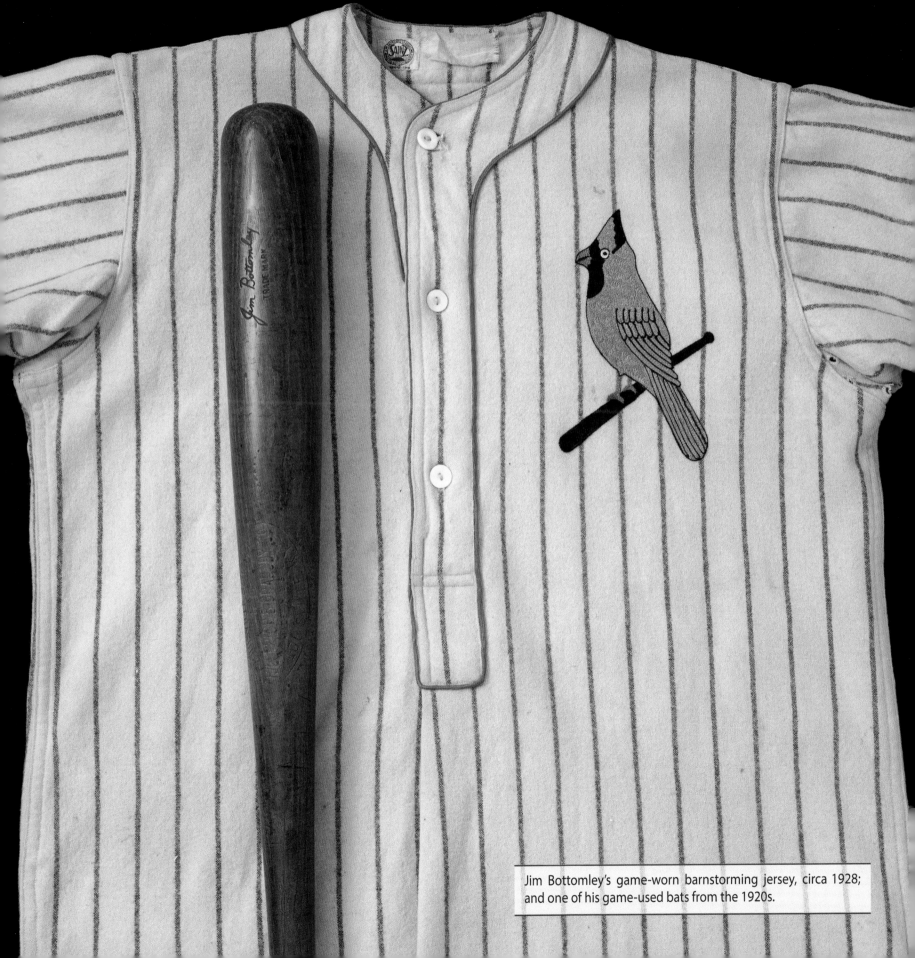

Jim Bottomley's game-worn barnstorming jersey, circa 1928; and one of his game-used bats from the 1920s.

The Cardinals uniform is one of the most iconic in sports, featuring the famous birds on the bat logo. The Museum has well over 200 jerseys, the oldest dating to 1919.

Grover Cleveland Alexander's 1926 regular-season game-worn road jersey; Billy Southworth's bat used by Jesse Haines to hit a home run in Game 3; a team-signed ball from the world champion Cardinals, also autographed by Babe Ruth; and the first pitched ball from the 1926 World Series.

1926 World Series

It was harvest time in St. Louis. The fruits of the farm system established by Branch Rickey in 1921 had ripened, bringing postseason baseball to Mound City for the first time since 1888.

Homegrown talent, led by the likes of Jim Bottomley, Ray Blades and Les Bell — coupled with player-manager Rogers Hornsby and the National League's Most Valuable Player, Bob O'Farrell — set the Cardinals on the winning path. But many credit the June acquisitions of outfielder Billy Southworth via trade and pitcher Grover Cleveland Alexander on a waiver claim from the Chicago Cubs as being the sparks that launched the Redbirds to the title. Alexander inherited this Eddie Dyer road jersey (opposite page) — previously used by the pitcher sent to the minors to create roster space for the 15-year veteran — and wore it until the team acquired new uniforms for the 1926 World Series.

The Cardinals had fallen to eight games off the pace in late May, but clawed their way back to take a half-game lead Aug. 20 and clinch the club's first National League pennant during the campaign's final weekend.

The inaugural pitch of the Fall Classic was thrown Oct. 2 from New York Yankees hurler Herb Pennock to Cardinals center fielder Taylor Douthit, who promptly drove the ball, pictured at left, to right field

for a double. Douthit later came around to score, but it would be the only Cardinals tally in a 2-1 loss. The Redbirds grabbed Game 2 behind Alexander's complete game, and the teams headed to St. Louis. Jesse Haines, the Cardinals' Game 3 starter, proved himself on the mound and at the plate, tossing a complete-game shutout and hitting a home run to help his cause. Haines swung this Billy Southworth model Kren's Special bat (opposite page) to stroke his fourth-inning bomb.

1926 World Series press pin

The Yankees roared back to take the next pair of games, forcing the Cardinals to win the final two contests at Yankee Stadium to claim the championship. On the heels of a second outstanding pitching performance by Alexander in Game 6, Hornsby again turned to his grizzled star hurler late in Game 7 to wrap up the title. Ahead by a lone run in the bottom of the seventh inning, "Old Pete" came on to strike out Tony Lazzeri with the bases loaded to preserve the lead. Alexander allowed just one runner the rest of the game — a walk to Babe Ruth with two outs in the bottom of the ninth. Ruth tried to steal second base, but O'Farrell gunned him down to end the Series and claim the first championship in Cardinals history.

Branch Rickey's 1926 World Series ring

"Jesse Haines, our pitcher, was the next man up, so I handed him his bat—he uses Southworth's. Haines connected with a good one and drove it into the right field bleachers for a home run. That was a wallop, and it sent the crowd nutty." – Ken Sullivan, 1926 Cardinals batboy

Frankie Frisch

It's never easy replacing a legend, especially one who hit over .400 three times and just managed his team to a world championship. But that's precisely the position Frankie Frisch found himself in when he was acquired by the Redbirds before the 1927 season. Nobody could replace Rogers Hornsby's mighty bat, but Frisch was a superstar in his own right.

Driven to prove the Hornsby trade wasn't a mistake, Frisch was runner-up for league Most Valuable Player honors during his first season in St. Louis. The switch-hitter finished 1927 among the National League's top 10 in hits, runs, triples, total bases and stolen bases. His 641 assists at second base that year still stands as the major league record for most assists by any player at any position in a single season.

Frisch's presence loomed large throughout the next several seasons, both on the field and in the clubhouse. The Cardinals captured two more NL pennants in 1928 and 1930, which may have been "The Fordham Flash's" best offensive season in St. Louis. He batted .346 and set career highs for runs batted in, doubles, on-base and slugging percentage. This road jersey (opposite page) with "St. Louis" on the front, worn by Frisch in 1930 or 1931—when the Cardinals won their second world championship—was the inspiration for the Cardinals' home alternate jersey introduced in 2013.

The second sacker's role as team leader was not lost on Branch Rickey, who named the 1931 National League Most Valuable Player as Cardinals player-manager in 1933. One year later, Frisch guided his club, the "Gas House Gang," to the top of the baseball world. It would mark Frisch's final appearance in the World Series, an event in which he played in eight times—four with the New York Giants and four with the Cardinals.

Frisch started at second base for the National League during the first two All-Star Games. He clubbed the National League's first-ever All-Star home run in the inaugural 1933 contest and went deep again to lead off the bottom of the first inning of the 1934 game. His All-Star career includes four hits in seven at-bats as a player, and a 4-1 defeat in his lone appearance as NL manager in 1935.

Frisch was tough as a dugout leader, valuing winning above all else and expecting his teammates to match his determination on the field. He continued in the dugout with the Cardinals through 1937, then managed another 10 seasons between the Pittsburgh Pirates and Chicago Cubs.

> *"Frisch was the best money player I ever saw. He could throw, he could field, he was smart, he knew how to play hitters, he was just a baseball player."* – Virgil "Spud" Davis, Cardinals catcher

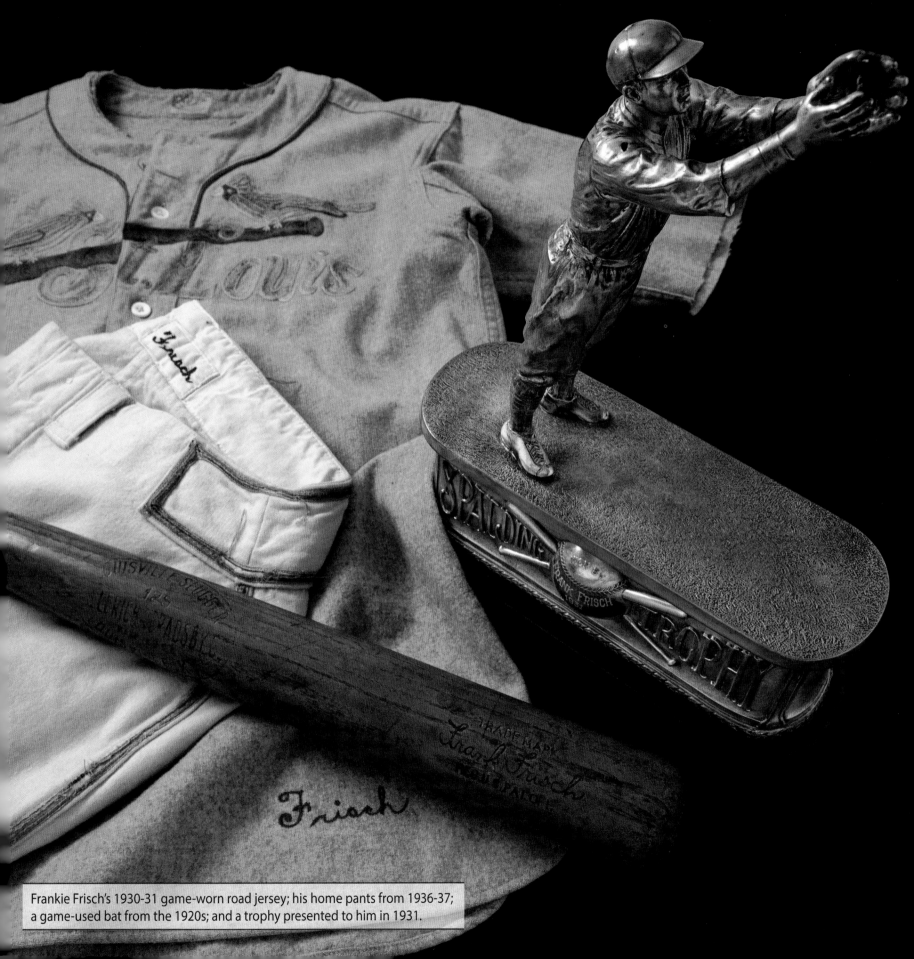

Frankie Frisch's 1930-31 game-worn road jersey; his home pants from 1936-37; a game-used bat from the 1920s; and a trophy presented to him in 1931.

Chick Hafey

Branch Rickey had a vision that the young pitcher he signed could be something special. Ironically, it was the player's vision—flawed by a chronic sinus problem—that prevented the eventual Hall of Famer from reaching his full potential and even greater acclaim.

Chick Hafey reported to spring training in 1923 determined to show off his tremendous arm. But, when Rickey saw the hurler also had a superb batting stroke and above-average speed on the bases, he realized Hafey's skills matched the blueprint for a quality outfielder. By late 1924, the former pitcher was roaming the grassy expanses of Sportsman's Park. After a rough start to the 1925 season and a trip back to the minors, Hafey went 4-for-5 in his first game back and batted .302 for the season.

Hafey's hitting prowess continued to grow, but he suffered constant vision problems in his left eye. In 1926, team physician Dr. Robert Hyland suggested that Hafey wear glasses to help, but evidence suggests the outfielder waited until 1929 to use corrective lenses in the field. Eventually, Hafey employed at least three pairs of glasses of varying strengths to accommodate his unpredictable sight.

Along with Jim Bottomley and Frankie Frisch, the "Three Musketeers" stabilized the Cardinals lineup and helped the club back to the World Series in 1928, 1930

and 1931. Hafey's finest offensive performance came during the 1931 campaign when he won the National League batting title with an average of .3489—besting New York's Bill Terry, who hit .3486. Toss in teammate Bottomley's .3481 average, and it was the closest three-way finish for a batting crown in baseball history.

The 1931 World Series would become Hafey's last in a Cardinals uniform. A salary holdout heading into spring training, just two years after another that had occurred before the 1930 season, triggered a trade to Cincinnati. Hafey played another five seasons with the Reds and recorded the first hit in the inaugural All-Star Game in 1933.

This 1929 Hafey jersey (opposite page) was made by the Sainz Athletic Company, a St. Louis garment-maker led by former Rawlings Athletic Company employee, Joseph Sainz. It's assumed that in an effort to win the Cardinals' business, Sainz provided new uniforms for the Cardinals to wear during the 1928 World Series, provided they would work with the company the following year. It marked the only season the Redbirds wore Sainz uniforms. Aside from that one season, the team dressed in both Spalding and Rawlings uniforms until 1932, when the club decided to work exclusively with Rawlings, cementing a relationship that lasted through the 2002 season.

"I always thought that if Hafey had been blessed with normal eyesight and good health, he might have been the best right-handed hitter baseball had ever known." – Branch Rickey

Chick Hafey's 1929 game-worn home jersey and an autograph book including his signature, along with other members of the Cardinals.

1931 World Series

The 1931 Cardinals had the recipe for success. They seized the National League lead on the last day of May and never relinquished it, posting the first 100-win season in franchise history and capturing the pennant by 13 games. Connie Mack's Philadelphia Athletics claimed the American League title by the same margin, setting up a rematch of the 1930 Fall Classic. To serve up a victorious dish over the reigning two-time world champions, the Cardinals would need a little more spice in the lineup.

They found it in the person of John Leonard "Pepper" Martin. Martin had labored in the Cardinals farm system for five years, earning a brief stint with the big club in 1928 and again in late 1930 after a standout season at Rochester. He made the Cardinals out of spring training in 1931 and established himself as the regular center fielder by mid-June, joining a lineup that boasted future Hall of Famers Jim Bottomley, Chick Hafey and that year's National League Most Valuable Player, Frankie Frisch.

Pepper Martin's regular-season statistics were unremarkable. He batted .300 in a league that hit .303 and ranked among league leaders in just two categories: stolen bases (16) and defensive assists in center field (10). In the 1931 World Series, though, he played like a man possessed, batting .500 with five stolen bases, five runs scored and five runs batted in. He tied a World Series record (since broken) with 12 hits, including four doubles and a home run. Excluding Pepper's exploits, the Cardinals batted an anemic .205. Few players before or since have dominated the World Series the way Martin did.

1931 World Series
press pin

The Cardinals were the only team to win back-to-back games during the Fall Classic, a see-saw affair that went the distance. Burleigh Grimes took a five-hit shutout into the ninth inning of Game 7 and was an out from victory before Philadelphia tallied twice, cutting the lead to 4-2. "Wild" Bill Hallahan, who gave up just one run in two complete-game starts in the Series, came on to nail down the final out, and the Redbirds ended the American League's streak of four consecutive World Series championships.

Among the artifacts featured here is a jersey (opposite page) that was worn by Game 4 starter Syl Johnson. The number 23 on the back indicates Johnson wore the garment in 1932 — the first year Cardinals players donned digits on the back. But, the lucky four-leaf clover sewn into the tail suggests the jersey was made for and worn during the 1931 World Series.

Earl "Sparky" Adams' 1931 World Series ring

> *"That's how the Series ended—the "Pepper Martin Series"—with a fly ball into the glove of the man himself."*
> – Bill Hallahan, Cardinals pitcher, on closing out the 1931 World Series

Syl Johnson's 1931 game-worn World Series home jersey; a team-signed baseball from the championship club; and a souvenir hat and miniature bat from the Fall Classic.

An authentic travel trunk used by the St. Louis Stars.

St. Louis Stars

A couple of years after Chris Von der Ahe's Brown Stockings began play in 1881, another team was launching organized Negro League baseball in the city. The St. Louis Black Stockings joined all-black teams from other cities — including Cincinnati, Cleveland and Louisville — in an effort to form a league. When the organization failed, the Black Stockings scheduled games against all-white clubs and booked their own nationwide tour. Even though they had great success on the field, the Black Stockings were forced to disband because keeping the franchise afloat financially was too difficult without the backing of a league.

The St. Louis Giants followed in the Black Stockings' footsteps, forming in 1909 and becoming a charter member of the Negro National League in 1920. Two seasons later, the club was sold and renamed the St. Louis Stars. The Stars were a successful franchise, winning league pennants in 1928, 1930 and 1931. The team featured some of the Negro League's biggest stars, including George Scales, George Giles, Ted "Highpockets" Trent, George "Mule" Suttles and Willie "Devil" Wells. No star shone brighter, though, than James "Cool Papa" Bell, a superb center fielder, outstanding leadoff hitter and one of the fastest runners to ever circle the base paths.

The Stars played in Stars Park, one of the few ballparks in America built explicitly for a Negro League team. Located on the grounds that today are home to Harris-Stowe State University's baseball diamond, Stars Park held 10,000 patrons and was

James "Cool Papa" Bell

adored by long-ball hitters who couldn't resist the short, left field wall — built just 269 feet from home plate to accommodate a trolley car barn.

Both the Stars and the Negro National League collapsed shortly after the 1931 season, casualties of the Great Depression. A new club with the same name, but few connections to the original Stars franchise, helped launch the Negro American League in 1937. Financial struggles caused the team to disband and reappear during the next few years, sometimes sharing hometown status with other cities. The Stars rejoined the Negro National League in 1943, but withdrew early in the season, bringing down the curtain on Negro Leagues baseball in St. Louis.

Authentic, period Negro Leagues memorabilia is very rare and desirable among sports collectors and museums. The Cardinals Museum has one of the finest collections of St. Louis-related Negro Leagues items known, even though the assemblage is relatively limited in size. This travel trunk (opposite page), featuring a hand-painted silhouette of a baseball player on a yellow star, is one of several pieces—including original programs, ticket stubs, autographed items and game-used balls — in the museum's collection.

The Cardinals have worn throwback uniforms honoring the Stars several times since 1997. In each instance, the jersey and cap designs were inspired by period photos since the team does not possess any original, game-worn Stars garments.

"Cool Papa was so fast, he could turn out the light and jump in bed before the room got dark." – Satchel Paige on the speed of Cool Papa Bell

Dizzy Dean

"I'm sorry, but I don't know you," said Branch Rickey. "Yes, you do. I'm the pitcher that struck out all them batters an' you asked me to stay in and strike out more. I'm Dean."

Dizzy Dean's introduction to Branch Rickey was hardly formal, but very memorable. Signed out of a tryout camp in 1930, he was called up to the big leagues that same year. In his only appearance, Dean tossed a complete-game shutout on the final day of the regular season. Following a year in the minors, Dizzy returned to St. Louis in 1932 with a bang, leading the league in both strikeouts and shutouts.

Dean was a force to be reckoned with, possessing a bite that was as big as his bark — and few barked

louder than ol' Diz. He was as tough on his employers and coaches as he was on opposing batters, frequently complaining about his pay and holding out for salary increases — a practice that infuriated the tight-pursed Rickey. He was money on the field, though, leading the league in complete games and innings pitched three times, and in wins on two occasions. Dean helped rally the club to the World Series

championship in 1934 with 30 wins in the regular season and two more in the Fall Classic.

Arguably the biggest draw in baseball after Babe Ruth, Dean was one of the first athletes to parlay his fame into advertising and entertainment deals. Following the 1934 World Series, he appeared on stages and radio shows across America, and even starred with brother Paul in an 18-minute Hollywood short. It's estimated Dizzy's income from endorsements and appearances that winter exceeded his baseball salary and bonuses by almost $10,000.

After his playing days were over, Dean returned to St. Louis as a colorful announcer for many years on both Cardinals' and Browns' broadcasts. Though he was in a Redbird uniform for parts of only seven seasons, he still ranks in the franchise top-10 in wins, complete games, shutouts and innings pitched, and remains third all-time in strikeouts behind Bob Gibson and Adam Wainwright.

Authentic Dizzy Dean game-used items are among the rarest of baseball memorabilia. His Louisville Slugger bat shipping records show only four bats were made for him during his career, and none of those have surfaced publicly. Four of his Cardinals jerseys are known to exist, with two belonging to the Cardinals Museum (opposite page). Both date to the 1936-37 period, distinguished by the two-color piping around the collar and placket. This feature, while subtle, was an expensive detail that wasn't continued beyond those two seasons.

"When ol' Diz was out there pitching, it was more than just another ballgame. It was a regular three-ring circus and everybody was wide-awake and enjoying being alive." – Les Bell, Cardinals infielder

Dizzy Dean's game-worn home and road jerseys from the 1936-37 seasons; a scorecard from July 30, 1933, when Dean set a then-MLB record of 17 strikeouts in a single game; and a "Me and Paul" box from an endorsed children's clothing line featuring the Dean brothers.

The trophy presented to Dizzy Dean by his team-mates for winning 30 games in 50 starts; a 1933-35 Leo Durocher game-worn home jersey; Joe Medwick's game-worn cap from the era; and a ticket and program from Game 5 of the World Series.

1934 World Series

In 1934, the Great Depression had sucked much of the life and fun out of the country. But, a wild and raucous troop of players with names like Dizzy, Ducky, Spud, Pepper, Ripper and The Lip would team up to take Cardinals fans on a memorable journey and put smiles on the faces of baseball buffs everywhere. The group was affectionately known as the "Gas House Gang" due to their dirty uniforms and all-out style of play. Reports vary, but most likely it wasn't until late in the season or in early 1935 when they were given the label.

1934 World Series press pin

The 1934 roster had evolved significantly since 1931; only Frank Frisch and Pepper Martin remained as regulars from the 101-win championship club. St. Louis' farm system provided a pipeline of major league-ready talent as six of the starting nine in Game 1 of the 1934 World Series were products of the club's minor league organization.

The squad played pretty average baseball throughout most of the season, even though five regulars batted better than .300. At times, they seemed more interested in playing pranks on one another, entertaining fans before games with circus-style catching drills, taking part in Vaudeville-type acts and instigating fights with teammates than in defeating the team across the diamond.

In late August, the Cardinals were trailing the New York Giants by seven games when Frisch lit a fire under his team. While the Giants stumbled, St. Louis went 21-7 in September and clinched the pennant on the last day of the season as Dizzy Dean won his 30th game. Teammates presented Dean the trophy featured here to mark his milestone victory. Dean and his brother, Paul — nicknamed "Daffy"— won a combined 49 games for the Redbirds.

Facing the heavily favored Detroit Tigers in the Fall Classic, the Gas House Gang rose to the occasion, taking the title in seven games, with the Dean brothers combining for all four wins. The Series is widely remembered for Joe Medwick's hard slide into Tigers third baseman Marv Owen in Game 7. A near riot followed and Medwick was removed from the game for his own safety. The play actually had little impact on the affair as the Cardinals cruised to an 11-0 win and their third World Series title.

Bill Delancey's 1934 World Series ring

"The Cardinals looked like a bunch of guys from the gashouse district who had crossed the railroad tracks for a game of ball with the nice kids."
– Joe Williams, writer for The New York World-Telegram, October 4, 1934

Clockwise from upper left: the first pitched ball from Opening Day at Busch III; a team-signed ball from the 1987 National League champions; a signed, gamed used ball from the five home run game against the Cubs in 2012; a hand-painted ball by noted folk-artist George Sosnak celebrating the 1967 world champions; Red Schoendienst's 1,000th win trophy ball; and a 1987 World Series game ball.

Clockwise from upper left: a 1927 team-signed baseball featuring Frank Frisch and Jim Bottomley; the first-pitched ball from Roger Dean Stadium, the Cardinals spring training complex; a 1941 team-signed baseball; the first home run hit in Busch Memorial Stadium; a game used ball from Michael Wacha's first Major League win and a ball commemorating Todd Worrell's Major League rookie saves record, illustrated by sports artist Amadee Wohlschlaeger.

Mud Cats Band

Following the trade of teammate and fellow prankster Ripper Collins to the Cubs, Pepper Martin needed a new outlet for his daily double dose of energy. He found it in a Christmas gift from his wife.

Pepper came to spring training in 1937 toting his regular baggage and a new toy — a guitar. He had been enamored with team trainer Doc Weaver's mandolin for years and thought he might like his own instrument, not appreciating the dexterity required to learn it. Martin labored for weeks trying to coax tunes from his new six-string, but "In Birmingham Jail" was the only song he vaguely "mastered" by the time he arrived at camp.

After Martin attempted to perform his tune for anyone who would listen, pitcher Bill McGee grabbed Pepper's guitar and began strumming chords. Other teammates joined in, exhibiting previously hidden musical talents. Soon, a small band formed — with Pepper relegated to the less-demanding harmonica. What began as a clubhouse diversion quickly grew into a musical act that, at times, took top billing over what happened between the baselines. Indeed, the Gas House Gang may have been baseball's most entertaining team both on and off the field.

The group called itself the Marvelous Musical Mississippi Mud Cats. Led by Martin, the oddball ensemble typically featured McGee on fiddle, Bob Weiland on the jug, Lon Warneke on guitar, Max Lanier on the harmonica and Frenchy Bordagaray stroking a washboard that included an auto horn and whistle. Lanier and Warneke shared the singing duties while Pepper bellowed out at certain points, offering directives such as "pizzicato," "obbligato" and "sweet po-tah-to!"

Martin once said, "We play everything — we play anything — whether we know it or not." They certainly weren't polished and were frequently concerned whether they would successfully end songs in unison. Still, the group gained a fair amount of renown playing a variety of country-western tunes and, in May 1937, was asked to perform on the Ripley's Believe It or Not national radio show.

The band wore outfits styled after western riding wear that mimicked the Cardinals' jerseys (opposite page); they featured a crest with two redbirds perched on a black bat and the words, "Mud Cats." Some accounts claim Martin tried to persuade Branch Rickey to create a baseball uniform with this logo, but the boss wouldn't oblige. The Mud Cats played anywhere and everywhere, striking up a tune on the train, at the hotel or even in the dugout. When the offseason arrived, the band booked concerts and made radio appearances across the country.

The act disbanded heading into the 1939 season because team management feared the players were distracted by their music and not focused enough on baseball. None of the musicians seemed terribly disappointed, though, recognizing their true talents were on the diamond.

"I was, perhaps, the only manager who carried an orchestra."
– Frank Frisch, Cardinals manager

Bob Weiland's original Marvelous Musical Mississippi Mud Cats outfit, along with Bill McGee's fiddle from his time with the famed ensemble.

Joe Medwick

In an era long before private gyms and personal trainers, "Muscles" was a physical specimen. A legitimate three-sport threat, the New Jersey native chose to take out his aggression on baseballs — along with anyone who didn't like the way he went about his business.

Joseph Michael Medwick was scouted by the Cardinals as a semipro outfielder in 1930 playing under the name "Mickey King." The all-state quarterback, who also was being wooed to play football for Notre Dame, used the alias to illicitly preserve his amateur status. Reportedly, two high school credits stood between Medwick and a scholarship offered by coach Knute Rockne. Instead of completing his academic coursework and heading to South Bend, Medwick signed with the Cardinals — but maintained the pseudonym in case he changed his mind. When Rockne died in a 1931 plane crash, Medwick dropped the fictitious name and committed to baseball full time.

Early in his career, he chose to go by "Mickey Medwick" and had that signature branded onto his Louisville Slugger bats (opposite page), for five seasons. Among friends and teammates, he preferred the nickname "Muscles," but it was a different handle that followed him the rest of his life. During Medwick's minor league days in Texas, a female fan wrote a letter to the Houston Post-Dispatch requesting more information about her favorite player, whom she called "Duckie" because "he walks just like a duck."

Most accounts claim that Medwick hated the moniker, yet he changed the signature on his Louisville Slugger bats in 1937 to read "Joe 'Ducky' Medwick."

By any name, Medwick was a force to be reckoned with in the batter's box. He led the league in doubles three times, hits twice and triples on one occasion. His greatest season came in 1937 when he won the Triple Crown — topping the senior circuit in batting average, home runs and runs batted in — and captured the National League Most Valuable Player Award. He also ranked first in runs, hits, doubles and total bases..

Medwick was fiercely proud of his accomplishments, but largely unapproachable. He loathed writers who wanted to interview him and detested fellow players who questioned any part of his game. Even teammates who were simply trying to help him out of a slump typically were met with resistance — and sometimes a punch.

His greatness on the field is often overshadowed by an incident that occurred in Game 7 of the 1934 World Series, when Medwick slid hard into Detroit Tigers' third baseman Marv Owen in the top of the sixth inning. Frustrated Detroit fans — whose team trailed the Cardinals 6-0 at that point — showered the playing field with fruit and debris when Medwick attempted to take his outfield position in the bottom of the inning. After a 17-minute delay, Commissioner Kenesaw Mountain Landis took Medwick out of the game for the left fielder's safety. Medwick was livid at the decision as he was one hit away from tying Pepper Martin's World Series record of 12 hits. But, an eventual 11-0 win and rowdy clubhouse celebration likely took the edge off his surly mood.

"He had very strong wrists and arms, and he could hit a ball as hard as anybody. And when he hit it, it just sailed." – Don Gutteridge, Cardinals infielder

One of the earliest-known examples of Medwick's professional bats, a "Mickey Medwick" model; Medwick's warm-up jacket from the 1930s, worn previously by fellow Hall of Famer Jim Bottomley; and the Babe Ruth Crown awarded to Medwick by the Maryland Professional Baseball Players Association in 1968, recognizing his 1937 Triple Crown season.

BABE RUTH CROWN
PRESENTED TO
JOE MEDWICK
FOR OUTSTANDING BATTING ACHIEVEMENT
1937
MARYLAND PROFESSIONAL BASEBALL PLAYERS ASSOCIATION

Johnny Mize

Johnny Mize batted over .400 during his two seasons playing for Piedmont College's varsity baseball team — even though he was still in high school. Piedmont's coach, whose school was unaffiliated with any conference and not bound by eligibility rules, convinced Branch Rickey to have a scout assess the young slugger. Rickey's brother, Frank, saw Mize play just one semipro game before signing the 17-year-old phenom.

The new recruit lacked the running speed needed to patrol the outfield, but his baseball IQ was well above average. Mize was moved to first base, where he later picked up the nickname, "The Big Cat," for his ability to dig underthrown balls out of the dirt. Offensively, Mize tore up the minors at every level, batting .336 over five-plus seasons.

Unfortunately for the young slugger, Cardinals first baseman Ripper Collins was in his prime — and in Mize's way. Collins led the National League in both home runs and OPS (on-base plus slugging percentage) in 1934 and put up similarly stellar numbers the following season, causing the club to sell Mize to Cincinnati for $55,000. An injured Mize, though, was unable to play, prompting the Reds to void the deal. It was a blessing in disguise for the Cardinals. Mize underwent successful surgery, made it to the big leagues in 1936 and beat out Collins for the first base job. Wielding lumber like this late-1930s Louisville Slugger (opposite page), he went on to place in the National League's top 10 in home runs, batting average, runs batted in, extra base hits, on-base percentage and slugging percentage during each of his six seasons in St. Louis.

Mize was Most Valuable Player Award runner-up in both 1939 and 1940, making him a prized trade chip for Rickey, who believed in moving players a year or two before their anticipated decline. This road jersey was worn by Mize during his final season with the Cardinals prior to being shipped to the New York Giants after the 1941 campaign. The trade turned out to be one of Rickey's rare missteps. Mize enjoyed several more outstanding seasons for the Giants and New York Yankees, ultimately earning a spot in the National Baseball Hall of Fame. The Big Cat's stay in St. Louis may have been cut prematurely short, but he still ranks second in batting average and 10th in home runs among modern-era Redbirds, and holds the club's single-season records for home runs and runs batted in by a left-handed hitter.

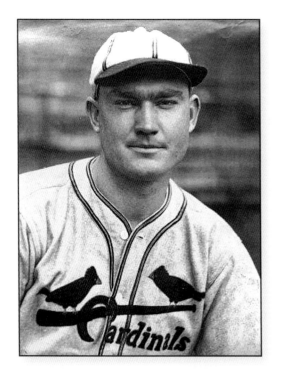

"Nobody had a better, smoother, easier swing than John. It was picture-perfect."
– Don Gutteridge, Cardinals infielder

Johnny Mize's game-worn road jersey from 1941, his final season with the Cardinals; and one of his wooden weapons, a Louisville Slugger from 1938-39.

Billy Southworth's 1942 game-worn World Series cap with modifications made by his son, who donned it while piloting bombers in World War II; and Southworth's reunion jersey worn for the 20th anniversary celebration of the Cardinals 1944 championship.

Billy Southworth

One of the most successful managers in Cardinals history, Billy Southworth experienced professional triumph and personal tragedy during his time in St. Louis. Both are represented in one of the museum's most interesting artifacts — a modified baseball cap.

When injuries derailed Southworth's 1927 season, he accepted an offer from Branch Rickey to become a player-manager in the farm system. After two successful years, he was called back to St. Louis to lead the big club. But, just 90 games into a disappointing 1929 season, Southworth was demoted back to the minors. By 1933, he was out of baseball.

Two seasons later, the Redbirds gave Southworth another chance, hiring him to manage one of their lower-level minor league squads. He worked his way up through the organization, polishing his credentials and managerial skills along the way, and found himself back in the Cardinals dugout in June 1940.

Southworth employed "small ball," pushing for one run at a time, and platooned players, a strategy that had fallen from favor in the National League. His methods worked for the talented Cardinals squad, which won a franchise-record 106 games in 1942 and defeated the heavily favored New York Yankees in the World Series. Southworth would lead the club to 105 wins and World Series appearances in each of the following two seasons, winning the championship again in 1944.

"The Little General's" son, Billy Southworth Jr., started his own baseball career as a minor league outfielder in 1936. When the 1940 season ended, he elected to become one of the first professional athletes to enlist in the military. The younger Southworth joined the Army Air Corps almost a year before Pearl Harbor was attacked and was called into action shortly after the 1942 Fall Classic concluded. His father gave him a good luck charm — his World Series cap.

Southworth's son made a few alterations to the hat to accommodate his piloting equipment and used it during some 25 bombing missions over Europe. He earned the Distinguished Flying Cross and Air Medal, and was promoted to bomb crew instructor upon his return stateside in 1944. On Feb. 15, 1945, during a routine training mission, Southworth Jr. died after his plane went down off the coast of New York. During this mission he left behind his lucky cap.

Southworth struggled profoundly after the loss of his son, and left St. Louis after the 1945 season. Though he managed the Redbirds in parts of only seven seasons, he is the lone skipper in club history to capture three 100-win seasons and two World Series championships.

"The cap has heard the roar of thousands of voices and the bark of 13 high-powered .50 caliber machine guns. Lucky for those who have worn it — it has ridden with a winner, always a champion." – From the wartime diary of Billy Southworth Jr.

Stan Musial's first home run ball, hit at Forbes Field September 23, 1941; and his 1942 contract, showing a salary of $750 a month.

IMPORTANT NOTICE

The attention of both Club and Player is specifically directed to the following excerpt from Major League Rule 3(a):

"No Club shall make a contract different from the uniform contract or a contract containing a non-reserve clause, except with the written approval of the Advisory Council. All contracts shall be in duplicate and the Player shall retain a counterpart original. The making of any agreement between a Club and Player not embodied in the contract shall subject both parties to discipline by the Commissioner; and no such agreement, whether written or verbal, shall be recognized or enforced by the Commissioner."

National League of Professional Baseball Clubs

UNIFORM PLAYER'S CONTRACT

Parties The ____ST. LOUIS NATIONAL BASEBALL CLUB____, herein called the Club, and ____STANLEY MUSIAL____, herein called the Player.

herein called the Club, and ____ of ____55 S. McKean Ave., Donora, Pa.____

Recital The Club is a member of the National League of Professional Baseball Clubs. As such, and jointly with the other members of the League, it is a party to the National League Constitution and to agreements and rules with the American League of Professional Baseball Clubs and its constituent clubs, and with the National Association of Professional Baseball Leagues. The purpose of these agreements and rules is to insure to the public wholesome and high-class professional baseball by defining the relations between Club and Player, between club and club, between league and league, and by vesting in a designated Commissioner broad powers of control and discipline, and of decision in case of disputes.

In view of the facts above recited the parties agree as follows:

Agreement
Employment 1. The Club hereby employs the Player to render skilled service as a baseball player in connection with all games of the Club during the year ____192____ including the Club's training season, the Club's exhibition games, the Club's playing season, and the World Series (or any other official series in which the Club may participate and in any receipts of which the player may be entitled to share) ; and the Player covenants that he will perform with diligence and fidelity the service stated and such duties as may be required of him in such employment.

2. For the service aforesaid the Club will pay the Player an aggregate salary of $____750.00____

Salary ____Seven hundred fifty dollars per month____, as follows:

In semi-monthly installments after the commencement of the playing season covered by this contract, unless the Player is "abroad" with the Club for the purpose of playing games, in which event the amount then due shall be paid on the first week-day after the return "home" of the Club, the terms "home" and "abroad" meaning, respectively, at and away from the city in which the Club has its baseball field.

If a monthly salary is stipulated above, it shall begin with the commencement of the Club's playing season (or such subsequent date as the Player's services may commence) and end with the termination of the Club's scheduled playing season, and shall be payable in semi-monthly installments as above provided.

If the Player is in the service of the Club for part of the playing season only, he shall receive such proportion of the salary above mentioned, as the number of days of his actual employment in the Club's playing season bears to the number of days in said season.

(a) The Player will faithfully serve the Club or any other Club to which, in conformity with the agreements above recited, this contract may be assigned, and pledges himself to the American public to conform to standards of personal conduct, of fair play and good sportsmanship.

The Player represents that he does not, directly or indirectly, own stock or have any financial interest in the ownership or earnings of any Major League club, except as hereinafter expressly set forth, and covenants that he will not hereafter, while connected with any Major League club, acquire or hold any such stock or interest in accordance with Major League Rule 20 (e).

(a) The Player agrees that, while under cont...
...son games as hereinafter stated) otherwise than fo...
in professional boxing or wrestling ; and that, exc...
not engage in any game or exhibition of football,...

(a) The Player agrees that, while under contract o...
except in conformity with the Major League Rules...
...n days after the close of the Major League champ...
...g training season, or in which more than two ot...
...ble player or team.

(a) In case of assignment of this contract to a...
...thin 72 hours from the date he receives written...
...iles by most-direct available railroad route, plus...
...shall be payable when he so reports ; and each su...
...during his term of service with such assignee,...
to report as above specified, he shall not be entitled to...
If the assignee is a member either of the National or...
specified. If the assignment, either outright or optional...

Stan Musial

Before he was "The Man," Stan Musial was a high school boy who hoped his fastball could help him escape the zinc mines of Pennsylvania.

A standout athlete in both basketball and baseball, Musial signed his first professional contract at the age of 16. His father desperately wanted him to go to college, and there had been some talk of a basketball scholarship. Baseball was Stan's first love, though, and he looked forward to joining the professional ranks after graduating. A few major league clubs had courted him, but he signed with the Cardinals due to their "salesmanship," and because the Pittsburgh Pirates, his favorite team growing up, never made an offer.

The southpaw posted a 9-2 record during his second minor league season in 1939, but interestingly, also batted .352. His skill with the lumber earned him time in the outfield when he wasn't pitching in 1940, and Musial didn't disappoint — his .311 average complemented an 18-5 record on the mound. Late in the season, though, while diving for a low line drive in center field, he jammed his left shoulder into the turf. The injury didn't affect his swing, but his days toeing the rubber had come to an end.

With a dedicated focus on hitting and fielding in 1941, Musial batted .379 and slammed 26 home runs in 87 games for his Class C Springfield (Illinois) club before getting called up to Rochester, just one level below the majors. The stiffer competition did little to slow the young slugger; in 54 games with the Red Wings, Musial hit .326, then headed home after the playoffs to rest and prepare for spring. The Cardinals had other plans; Musial received a wire telling him to report to St. Louis.

The Redbirds were in a pennant race when Stan arrived on September 17. He was issued uniform No. 6 and saw his first action during the second game of a doubleheader that day, recording two hits. A week later, the team hit the road for a matchup in Pittsburgh. Playing at Forbes Field, where he had cheered on the Pirates as a boy, Stan clubbed his first major league home run. A group of supporters from Musial's hometown of Donora had come to cheer him on, including his friend, Steve Posey. Stationed in the right-field seats, Posey caught Musial's long ball (opposite page), and traded it to the rookie in exchange for a new one. Musial appeared in 12 games for the Cardinals that September, hitting safely in 10 of them and batting .426.

"Good fastball, curve fair. Nice poise, big boy. He can hit and may be too good a hitter to keep out of the game."
– Report from Cardinals scout Wid Matthews on Musial following the 1940 season

1942 World Series

If the 1926 world championship proved the Cardinals farm system's worth, the 1942 title confirmed its dominance. On a roster that recorded 106 wins, a franchise record, every player but two had come up through or spent time in St. Louis' minor league organization.

In spite of the impressive victory total, the Redbirds didn't claim the pennant until the final day of the season. The club spent most of the year looking up at the Brooklyn Dodgers, which sat alone atop the standings for five months. Trailing by 10 games on August 5, St. Louis won 31 of its next 39 games to catch the Dodgers, then went 12-2 down the stretch to secure the title. Strong pitching made the difference those final weeks, led by Mort Cooper and Johnny Beazley, who each finished with more than 20 wins.

Cooper especially stood out. After a 2-3 start to the season, he won nine straight decisions from mid-May through June. When he struggled to notch his 14th victory, Cooper — not known to be superstitious — switched from his customary uniform number 13 to 14 for his August 14 start. He tossed a two-hit shutout, beginning a dominant run in which he won 10 of his final

1942 World Series press pin

11 starts. Nine of those wins were complete games, including a crucial 14-inning, 2-1 win over Brooklyn on August 25. Along the way, Cooper switched uniform numbers each start to coincide with the win he was chasing. He finished the season with a league-leading 22 wins, 10 shutouts, a 1.78 earned run average and the National League's Most Valuable Player Award.

Enos Slaughter paced the Cardinals in most offensive categories, but the difference between losing to the Dodgers by $2^{1/2}$ games in 1941 and edging them by two games in 1942 may have been the addition of rookie Stan Musial. In his first full season in the majors, Musial finished third in the National League in both batting average (.315) and triples (10), and fourth in slugging percentage (.490).

The momentum that built throughout the second half of the season — in which the team went 63-11 — carried into the World Series. Facing a powerful New York Yankees squad that had captured 103 victories itself, the Cardinals wrapped up the Fall Classic in only five games, winning the final four contests after dropping the opener.

Johnny Hopp's 1942 World Series ring

"I played on a lot of good ballclubs, but the '42 team was the best I ever played on. We had everything. We had good pitching, good defense and good hitting, even though we were not particularly a running team or a power team."

– Marty Marion, Cardinals shortstop

Harry Walker's 1942 game-worn home jersey, featuring the "HEALTH" patch in support of the Hale America Fitness Campaign; a championship belt buckle inscribed to Stan Musial; a team-signed baseball; a pass issued to service members at the Jefferson Barracks Military Post; and Terry Moore's game-used glove.

MVP Awards

For more than 100 years, various entities have recognized the best ballplayers in Major League Baseball. The ultimate accolade for individual success is the Most Valuable Player Award, known previously as the League Award. Sixteen different Cardinals have claimed the honor, with Stan Musial and Albert Pujols each receiving it three times.

Winners of the League Award, which was presented in the National League from 1924 through 1928, earned a cash prize and a bronze medal for being "the greatest all-around service to his club."

The Baseball Writers Association of America (BBWAA) began voting for the Most Valuable Player Award in each league in 1931. This award is recognized by Major League Baseball as the official MVP honor. It was named the "Kenesaw Mountain Landis Memorial Baseball Award" following the death of baseball's first commissioner in 1944.

The Cardinals Museum has examples of both awards, including Bob O'Farrell's League Award from 1926, Marty Marion's Most Valuable Player Award from 1944 — the first year it was named after Commissioner Landis — and all three of Stan Musial's plaques.

St. Louis Cardinals Most Valuable Player Award Winners

The League Award (1924–29)

- 1925 - Rogers Hornsby
- 1926 - Bob O'Farrell
- 1928 - Jim Bottomley

The National League Most Valuable Player Award (1931–present)

- 1931 - Frank Frisch
- 1934 - Dizzy Dean
- 1937 - Joe Medwick
- 1942 - Mort Cooper
- 1943 - Stan Musial
- 1944 - Marty Marion

- 1946 - Stan Musial
- 1948 - Stan Musial
- 1964 - Ken Boyer
- 1967 - Orlando Cepeda
- 1968 - Bob Gibson
- 1971 - Joe Torre
- 1979 - Keith Hernandez*
- 1985 - Willie McGee
- 2005 - Albert Pujols
- 2008 - Albert Pujols
- 2009 - Albert Pujols

*co-MVP with Willie Stargell

Bob O'Farrell's 1926 League Award Medal

"I look at that trophy and I know I was consistent. For one year I can say I was one of the best baseball players in the world."
– Willie McGee on winning the 1985 NL MVP

NATIONAL LEAGUE ★ CHAMPIONS *St. Louis* ★ CARDINALS • 1967

NELSON BRILES
STEVE CARLTON
BOB GIBSON
JOE HOERNER
HAL WOODESHICK
TIM McCARVER
DAVE RICKETTS
JOHN ROMANO
ED BRESSOUD
ORLANDO CEPEDA
PHIL GAGLIANO

AL JACKSON
LARRY JASTER
RAY WASHBURN
RON WILLIS

DICK HUGHES

JULIAN JAVIER
DAL MAXVILL
MIKE SHANNON
ED SPIEZIO
BOB TOLAN

LOU BROCK
CURT FLOOD
ALEX JOHNSON
ROGER MARIS

RED SCHOENDIENST

St. Louis CARDINALS

NEW BUSCH MEMORIAL STADIUM

100TH
1892 1992
ANNIVERSARY
ST. LOUIS CARDINALS

ST. LOUIS CARDINALS

Busch Stadium
St. Louis Missouri

St. Louis Cardinals

Busch Stadium

1938 ST. LOUIS **CARDINALS**

Louis dinal

L. Smith
Ramsey
Oberkfell
Gonzalez
Porter
Tenace
Iorg
Landrum
Green
McGee
Hendrick
Braun
O. Smith
Herr
Forsch
Martin
Littell
Kaat
Hernandez
Mura
LaPoint
Bair
Sutter
Rincon
Lahti

ST. LOUIS CARDINALS

MGR. HERZOG

WORLD CHAMPIONS 1982

Cardinals

CARDINALS

St. Louis **CARDINALS**

Souvenir WORLD SERIES

ST. LOUIS **CARDINALS** 1944

WORLD SERIES CHAMPIONS 20.06

Cardinals

WORLD SERIES 2006

The Museum collection includes over 175 pennants that have lauded everything from new ballparks to club milestones to World Series championships, and everything in between.

Gene Moore's 1944 Browns home jersey; Danny Litwhiler's 1944 Cardinals reunion jersey from 1964; George McQuinn's home run bat from Game 1 of the World Series; NL MVP Marty Marion's game-used bat; ticket stubs from World Series Games 1 and 5; and matching pennants from the Streetcar Series.

1944 World Series

St. Louisans received an unexpected gift in 1944 as both of the city's major league franchises won their league pennants and faced off in the World Series.

It wasn't unexpected for the Cardinals to be in this position. They notched more than 100 wins for the

1944 Browns
World Series press pin

1944 Cardinals
World Series press pin

third straight season — a National League record — and were either tied for or alone in first place after all but three games during the entire 1944 campaign. The Cardinals recorded just 112 errors during the season — another league record — and saw their shortstop, Marty Marion, claim Most Valuable Player honors. It was the third straight year a Redbird earned the award.

The Browns, in contrast, had never qualified for postseason play and recorded just one winning record since 1929. The club finished the 1943 season in sixth place, 25 games off the pace. But, the 1944 Browns started off red-hot, winning their first nine games, an American League record at the time. While most teams in the Junior Circuit struggled with the loss of key players to World War II service, the Brownies roster remained essentially intact. Solid pitching carried them to the league crown; four of the team's five starters posted double-digit win totals and the staff brought a 3.17 earned run average into the Series.

Even though St. Louis had primarily been a Cardinals town for some time — thanks to the club's consistent success since the 1920s — some accounts suggested there was a groundswell of support for the underdog Browns. Coined the "Streetcar Series" because thousands of fans took the Grand Avenue Streetcar to get to Sportsman's Park, it would be the last World Series played entirely in one ballpark.

George McQuinn homered in the fourth inning of Game 1 using this bat (opposite page), driving in both runs in the Browns' 2-1 victory. The surprising Browns took two of the first three games, outscoring the Cardinals 10-6 in those contests. But the Redbirds' pitching took over, allowing their rivals just two runs in the final three games to secure the title.

The Browns' first World Series would prove to be their last. In 1945, playing without Stan Musial — who was serving in the Navy — the Cardinals came within three games of making five straight World Series appearances. They would return to the Fall Classic in 1946.

Johnny Hopp's
1944 Cardinals
World Series ring

Browns part-owner
Samuel McCluney's
1944 American League
Championship ring

"Everybody thought we had a better club, and we did too. But that was one of the toughest Series we played. They played tough, and we were always having to play catch-up." – Stan Musial, Cardinals outfielder in the 1944 World Series

Enos Slaughter

He is remembered as a product of the Gas House Gang-era Cardinals — a gritty competitor, brilliant outfielder and hustling base runner who dashed his way into Redbirds lore.

Enos Slaughter was signed by the Redbirds as a heavy-hitting, but lumbering, second baseman. He grabbed the Cardinals' attention during a minor league tryout supervised by Billy Southworth, who suggested the flat-footed slugger try running on his toes. Slaughter obliged and soon discovered he could sprint from home plate to first base a good four steps faster than before. Just as importantly, he was able to cover more ground defensively, enabling a shift to the outfield.

Nicknamed "Country" because of his upbringing in rural North Carolina, Slaughter spent three seasons in the minors before making the St. Louis roster out of spring training in 1938. The 22-year-old right fielder proved he belonged, batting a respectable .276 in 112 games. By 1939, the time he spent in the minors working on his speed and outfield skills began to pay dividends. Offensively, he led the National League with 52 doubles and batted .320; defensively, no Senior Circuit outfielder recorded more putouts, assists or double plays. Slaughter made the first of 10 All-Star appearances in 1941 and was runner-up in 1942 National League Most Valuable Player Award

voting after leading the league in hits, triples and total bases.

Just days after celebrating the team's 1942 world championship, Slaughter enlisted in the Air Force. His military service kept him out of the game three years, but when he returned for the 1946 season, it was like he never left. Slaughter hit .300 and led the league with 130 runs batted in on the way to another pennant. His career-defining moment came during Game 7 of the 1946 World Series. With two outs and the score tied 3-3 in the bottom of the eighth inning, Slaughter broke from first on a double by Harry Walker and never hesitated, beating Johnny Pesky's relay throw home. His "mad dash" around the bases scored the go-ahead run, which ultimately decided the game and the Series.

Two days before the start of the 1954 campaign, Slaughter — the unofficial captain of the club — was traded to the New York Yankees to create playing time for Wally Moon, who became that season's Rookie of the Year. "Country" was blindsided by the deal and, along with Stan Musial, openly cried at the news. When he was dealt, Slaughter stood as the franchise leader in games played and runs batted in. Today, he still ranks among the club's top five in triples, runs batted in, walks, games played, at-bats, runs, hits and total bases.

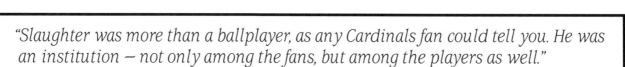

"Slaughter was more than a ballplayer, as any Cardinals fan could tell you. He was an institution — not only among the fans, but among the players as well."
– Bob Burnes in the St. Louis Globe-Democrat after Slaughter's 1954 trade to the Yankees

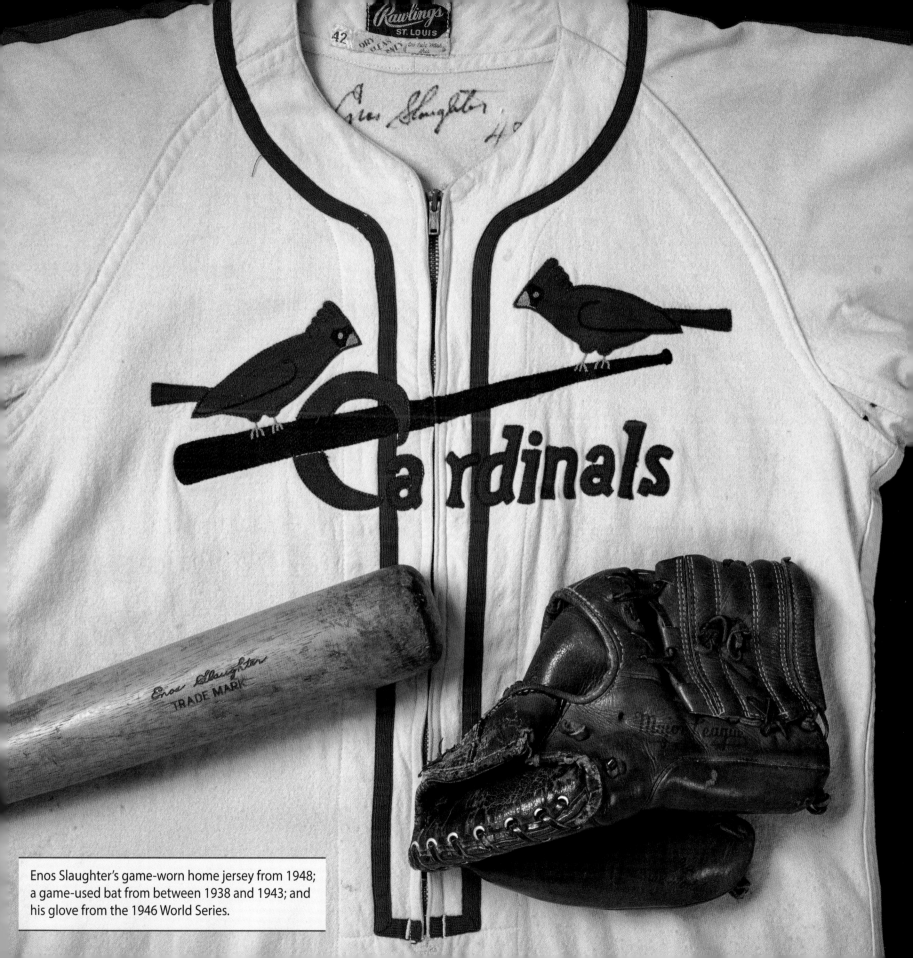

Enos Slaughter's game-worn home jersey from 1948;
a game-used bat from between 1938 and 1943; and
his glove from the 1946 World Series.

1946 World Series

With World War II at an end, Americans welcomed home the many men and women who had served their country around the globe. Included in that group were Cardinals stars Stan Musial and Enos Slaughter. It would have been reasonable to expect these two returning servicemen to need some time to

1946 World Series press pin

get back into the rhythm of the game, especially since neither was discharged until a few weeks before opening day. However, both picked up exactly where they left off.

Musial reminded opposing pitchers how dominant he could be by leading the league in batting average, runs, hits, doubles, triples and total bases. His .365 average ultimately would rank as the second-highest of his illustrious career. No slouch himself, Slaughter led the league with a career-high 130 runs batted in and placed third in the National League home run chase. The duo finished first and third, respectively, in National League Most Valuable Player Award voting.

The pitching staff was led by the arms of Howie Pollet — whose 21 wins, 2.10 earned run average and 266 innings pitched were tops in the league — and Harry Brecheen, who posted 15 wins and a league-best five shutouts.

The Redbirds entered the final weekend of the campaign with a slim one-game lead over the

1946 World Series program

Brooklyn Dodgers, but dropped two of three games to the Chicago Cubs and ended the season in a dead heat. The two 96-win teams squared off in the first playoff series in Major League history, a best-of-three affair. The Redbirds swept the first two games from the Dodgers to claim the pennant.

Waiting in the World Series were the 104-win Boston Red Sox and their star, Ted Williams. The much-anticipated clash of titan sluggers — Musial and Williams — was a disappointment as each batted less than .225. The Series itself, though, was exciting and hard-fought, with the teams trading victories through the first six games. In the decisive seventh game, with the scored tied 3-3 in the eighth inning, Slaughter took off from first on a double by Harry Walker and surprised Boston by circling the bases to put the Cardinals ahead. His "mad dash" would prove to be the winning run as Brecheen closed the door on the Red Sox in relief for his third victory in three appearances. The Redbird southpaw finished with a 0.45 earned run average over 20 innings and was the first pitcher since 1920 to win three games in a World Series. The Cardinals claimed their third world championship in five years and the Sixth in franchise history.

"A 3-2 pitch, two men out. I was running on the play when Harry Walker hit this little looping ball into left-center. As I rounded second, I said to myself, 'I can score.'"
– Enos Slaughter on his "mad dash" in Game 7 of the 1946 World Series

Stan Musial's 1946 game-worn home jersey; Terry Moore's glove from the Fall Classic; Enos Slaughter's cleats from the period; a 1946 team-signed ball.

Eddie Gaedel

Famed owner and showman Bill Veeck bought the St. Louis Browns in 1951 and immediately set out to be a thorn in the side of the Cardinals. His intention was to win over local fans and run the Redbirds out of town. But it would be an uphill battle considering the Cardinals had accumulated six world championships the previous 25 years and featured a player named Musial. Ticket sales and winning went hand-in-hand, and the Browns had not experienced much of either.

Shortly after taking ownership of the team that July, Veeck wanted to put his stamp on the new operation. Part of his strategy involved pioneering stadium giveaways and between-inning entertainment to get spectators engaged. On Grandstand Manager's Day, for example, he allowed a group of fans to direct the game from the stands. No stunt was more memorable, though, than the pinch-hitting appearance of 3-foot-7-inch Eddie Gaedel.

After the first game of a doubleheader on August 19, 1951—in which fans received a piece of birthday cake and ice cream to celebrate the 50th anniversary of the American League—an oversized faux birthday cake was rolled onto the field while various circus-style acts performed at each base. The public address announcer told the crowd, "Ladies and gentlemen, as a special birthday present to manager Zack Taylor, the management is presenting him with a brand-new Brownie." At that point, Gaedel, clad in an official Browns uniform, jumped out of the cake.

Most, if not all, of the announced crowd of 18,000 thought the stunt was over—including some visibly annoyed executives of the Falstaff Brewery, who were sponsoring the big day. But Veeck had something bigger up his sleeve. In the bottom of the first inning, Browns leadoff man Frank Saucier was pulled back and Gaedel was sent in to hit for him. Tigers manager Red Rolfe immediately summoned the umpire, who turned to the Browns manager. Taylor was prepared; he presented a copy of Gaedel's one-day contract to the arbiter and play resumed. Gaedel walked on four straight pitches, then was lifted for a pinch runner after reaching first base.

Veeck received the national attention he craved but also raised the ire of American League President William Harridge, who was so upset about the stunt that he changed the way player contracts were approved.

One element that helped make the occasion so grandiose was Veeck's use of a fraction on Gaedel's jersey. Major League uniforms sized for children or little people were not readily available in 1951 as they are today, so to prepare for the event, Veeck borrowed the batboy uniform from the general manager's son and replaced the number 6 on the back with the fraction "1/8." The batboy, Billy DeWitt Jr., would grow up to become the principal owner and CEO of the Cardinals.

"You'll be appearing before thousands of people. Your name will go into the record books for all time. You'll be famous, Eddie. You'll be immortal."
– Bill Veeck to Eddie Gaedel before his pinch-hit appearance

Cardinals owner Bill DeWitt Jr.'s batboy uniform, worn by Eddie Gaedel during his famous pinch-hit appearance for the St. Louis Browns.

Hidden in plain sight: Gaedel's uniform number was printed in the official scorecard that day, a detail overlooked by many fans.

⅛—Gaedel
2—Marsh, if
3—Arft, if
5—Young, if
6—Jennings, if
8—B. Taylor, if
9—Lollar, c
10—Batts, c
11—Maguire, of
12—Wood, of
1⁵—Byrne, p
16—Saucier, of
18—Sanford, p
20—Widmar, p
21—Pillette, p

2921 Meramec St.,
St. Louis 18, Mo.,
April 15, 1953

Mr. August A. Busch, Jr.,
Anheuser-Busch, Inc.,
721 Pestalozzi Street,
St. Louis, Missouri

Dear Mr. Busch:--

First of all let me congratulate you on the purchase of my favorite base-ball team "The Cardinals". Believe me when I say I was heart-sick when I read that the Cardinals were likely to be sold to another city and then when your wonderful company made the wise choice of buying them I was thrilled. I am even more thrilled to hear of your purchase of Sportsmans Park and the name you have selected to call it.

However, I have a suggestion to make that I think is worth turning over to your Ways & Means Committee to be discussed at your next Board Meeting.

It cost a great deal of money to purchase the Cardinals, the ball park and the intended renovations you plan on making which is wonderful. My suggestion is this, why not go back to the old days when they had "Ladies Day"?

At the present time, if my husband wants to take his family to the ball-game in style, we have to save for a month. We are the typical American family, husband, wife, and boy 12 and a girl 8, who are just at the right age to understand base-ball. It will cost us at least $10.00 and believe me it is just too expensive for one afternoon, however, we do manage to go at least once on our vacation.

If you would have a Ladies Day and charge 25¢ for the wife and children, think how many families would be on hand, and even during the summer weeks think how many mothers would take their children to the ball game. I can remember when I had my work all finished and be out to the ball park 1/2 hour before the game started. But now I am lucky to go once a season and that is as a sponsor with my church group. Think of all the Girl Scouts and Boy Scouts and their leaders and sponsors who would bring their troops out and other groups too numerous to mention. Those seats are available so you might as well have some one sitting in them.

Of course this is just one woman's opinion but I think it is a good one and worth talking about as well as doing it.

Think of the boom in your business when the ladies were introduced to the fine flavor of "BUDWEISER", and that same thing will happen to base-ball.

There's nothing like it, absolutely nothing.

Sincerely,
Mrs. W. Robert Witte

MW:self

H. H. HUMMEL, PRES.

CHestnut 2998

Sporting Goods Company, Inc.
1114 LOCUST STREET
ST. LOUIS 1, MISSOURI

April 17, 1953

Mr August Busch, President
St Louis Cardinals
Grand and Dodier Street
St Louis Missouri

Dear Mr Busch:

With the opening of the 1953 baseball season in St. Louis, we wish you every success as President of the St. Louis Cardinals Baseball Club.

It is our sincere belief that your interest and association with the already famous and beloved Red Birds can only lend ably to their future achievements and greatness. As baseball fans we are grateful and happy, as St Louisians we commend you, and proudly extend our wishes for your every success as the head of a grand institution, the St Louis Cardinals Baseball Club.

Sincerely Yours,
SISLER HUMMEL SPORTING GOODS COMPANY, INC.,
Per Harold H. Hummel
Harold H. Hummel
PRESIDENT-TREASURER

MOtt Haven 9-4411

The Sporting News

Publishers Since 1886

THE SPORTING GOODS DEALER • THE SPORTING GOODS TRADE DIRECTORY • THE SPORTING NEWS
THE SPORTING GOODS DEALER'S NEWSLETTER
THE QUARTERBACK • FOOTBALL PRO RECORD AND RULE BOOK • BASEBALL REGISTER • THE SPORTING NEWS RECORD BOOK • THE BASEBALL GUIDE
DOPE BOOK • ONE FOR THE BOOK • HOW TO PLAY
HOW TO SCORE • READY RECKONER • THE REAL BABE RUTH • THE ALL-SPORTS NEWS

CHestnut 5400
2018 Washington Avenue
ST. LOUIS 3, MO.

April 15, 1953

CHARLES C. SPINK, Founder
J. G. TAYLOR SPINK, General Manager
C. C. SPINK, Advertising Director

NEW YORK 17 . . . . 535 FIFTH AVE.
CHICAGO 11 . . . . 520 N. MICHIGAN AVE.
CLEVELAND 21 . . . . 1199 DORR ROAD
DETROIT 6 . . . . PENOBSCOT BLDG.
LOS ANGELES 14 . . . . 3156 WILSHIRE BLVD.
SAN FRANCISCO 4 . . . . 300 MONTGOMERY ST.
BOSTON 10 . . . . 140 FEDERAL STREET

Mr. August A. Busch,
Anheuser-Busch Inc.,
721 Pestalozzi,
St. Louis, Mo.

My dear Mr. Busch:

In order that you may have a record of the service units which received copies of the Official Baseball Guide with the compliments of your club, we are enclosing cards listing these units. Three hundred copies of the Guides were mailed to this list two weeks ago.

As you will observe, a thorough distribution was made, and many servicemen will have access to the Guides, as a result. We are certain the books will add to their enjoyment of the season and their interest in baseball.

We appreciate the opportunity you gave us to provide these [Guid]es for so many servicemen.

Sincerely yours,
J.G.Taylor Spink

JGTS:FS

Attention: Public Relation Director

Dear Sir:

As my fourteen year old son is an ardent St. Louis Cardinal "booster", it is his desire to be the proud owner of a genuine Cardinal Baseball Cap. It would be greatly appreciated by him, if you could forward one cap (size: 7¼) to the address listed below.

If there should be any charges, kindly bill me direct.

Wishing you a successful season...1953.

Sincerely,
Orien E. McDaniel
Orien E. McDaniel

Address:

Orien McDaniel, Jr.,
128 South Broadway
White Plains, New York

Letters delivered to August A. Busch Jr. following
the brewery's purchase of the Cardinals in 1953.

New York Post

August A. Busch Jr.

After owning the club for more than a quarter-century, a terminally ill Sam Breadon hand-picked Fred Saigh to be his successor. Saigh dearly loved owning the Cardinals but a controversial tax-evasion conviction and resulting pressure from the league to sell the team forced his hand just six years into his tenure. Rejecting more-lucrative offers from investors in Houston and Milwaukee, Saigh sold the Cardinals to Anheuser-Busch for $3.75 million in 1953, ensuring the Redbirds would remain in St. Louis.

August A. Busch Jr., the animated head of the brewery, assumed the role of team president. At the time, "Gussie" was a casual baseball fan who had to be convinced by executives in his inner circle that purchasing the Redbirds would enhance the company's brand and make him a civic hero. Little did they realize how right they would be; Anheuser-Busch became America's top brewer within four years of acquiring the Cardinals.

Browns owner Bill Veeck didn't have the finances to compete with the brewery or to improve Sportsman's Park—which the Cardinals had rented from the Browns for more than three decades. So he sold the ballpark to Anheuser-Busch for $800,000 and moved his team to Baltimore in 1954. Ever the marketer, Busch decided to rename the ballpark "Budweiser Stadium." Some fans, local groups and fellow owners objected to naming the facility after a product, and an alcoholic beverage, at that. In response, just 24 hours after his pronouncement, Gussie rechristened the park "Busch Stadium" in memory of his father, grandfather and brother. The new owners then invested $1.5 million to upgrade every aspect of the ballpark, which had fallen into disrepair.

By the late 1950s, in spite of improvements, the Cardinals' aging stadium had become obsolete and in need of replacement. Parts of the inner city were also suffering from urban decay. A solution to both problems was proposed in 1959—a new, downtown, multipurpose sports stadium surrounded by hotels, restaurants, shops and parking. Busch spearheaded the effort.

The Cardinals delivered a world championship for Busch in 1964 before leaving Sportsman's Park, then repeated the feat three years later in the downtown stadium's second season. It took 15 years before Busch would see his Redbirds claim another world championship in 1982. The team returned to the World Series twice more before Gussie's death in 1989.

Anheuser-Busch sold the Cardinals to the Bill DeWitt Jr.-led ownership group in 1996, but still owns the naming rights to the current stadium and maintains a close relationship with the club. Gussie's fingerprints remain on the franchise as well. Number 85 was retired in honor of his 85th birthday in 1984; his beloved Budweiser Clydesdales take a lap around the field every opening day; and the Anheuser-Busch jingle he adored, "Here Comes the King," is a staple of the stadium organist after the seventh inning.

"Development of the Cardinals will have untold value for our company. This is one of the finest moves in the history of Anheuser-Busch."
– August A. Busch Jr., speaking to the Anheuser-Busch board of directors regarding the purchase of the St. Louis Cardinals

Rogers Hornsby's game-worn road managerial jersey from 1952; bats used by Ken Williams and John Tobin during the 1920s; and George Sisler's game-worn first baseman's mitt from the 1920s.

St. Louis Browns

Four years after the city's National League team last took the field as the "Browns," a second professional club came to town and adopted the familiar name. The Milwaukee Brewers were an original member of the American League in 1901 but after just one season, the franchise moved to St. Louis and became the Browns. The team finished in second place in 1902 with a .574 winning percentage, a mark that would be topped by only the 1922 and 1944 clubs.

Branch Rickey originally came to St. Louis as part of the Browns organization and signed a young man — one he had previously managed at the University of Michigan — who would become the greatest player in club annals. George Sisler was a speedy, slick-fielding first baseman who is one of only two players in American League history to hit .400 or better twice. Sisler led the Browns to one of their finest seasons in 1922 when they won a franchise-record 93 games, falling just one short of the pennant. He posted a .420 batting average and led the American League in hits and runs scored while teammate Ken Williams led the circuit in round-trippers and runs batted in. That year, Williams became the first big leaguer to hit 30 home runs and steal 30 bases in the same season.

In spite of its reputation as a perennial loser — the franchise recorded just 11 winning seasons during its 52 years in St. Louis — the Browns were arguably more popular locally than the Cardinals during the club's first two decades. As the team's fortunes improved in the mid-1920s, owner Phil Ball nearly doubled the seating capacity of Sportsman's Park in anticipation of someday hosting a World Series. But it was the Redbirds —tenants of the Browns since 1920 — that brought home the first world championship in 1926 and, in the process, began turning St. Louis into a Cardinals town.

In 1944, when most other teams had lost multiple players to military service, the Browns roster remained essentially intact. With experience on its side, the club edged out Detroit for the Browns' first American League pennant and a date in the World Series with their Sportsman's Park counterparts. The surprising Browns grabbed two of the first three games but the Cardinals' superior pitching took over from there and allowed only two runs in the final three contests to secure the title. The "Streetcar Series" was the last World Series to be played entirely in one ballpark.

After World War II ended, the Browns never finished higher than sixth place and struggled to sell tickets. Anheuser-Busch's purchase of the Cardinals in 1953 caused Browns owner Bill Veeck to surrender any notion of competing off the field with the other local team so he sold the franchise, which moved to Baltimore and became the Orioles in 1954.

"More of the fans were rooting for us because the Cardinals were supposed to kill us."
– Ellis Clary, Browns infielder in the 1944 World Series

Tom Alston

When Gussie Busch attended his first game as Cardinals owner in 1953, Jackie Robinson had already played six seasons for the Brooklyn Dodgers.

St. Louis had a larger nonwhite population than any other major league city but as the southernmost outpost in either league, attitudes regarding the racial divide had been slow to evolve. The new owner was determined to change that, saying, "Baseball is supposed to be the great American national game and there is no room for discrimination in it."

Less than three months after Busch purchased the club, the Cardinals inked Leonard Tucker, the first African-American in franchise history. Tucker was a solid player, but a low-level prospect. Seeking more immediate results, some accounts maintain Busch offered New York Giants owner Horace Stoneham $1 million for Willie Mays. His overtures were rebuffed, much to Busch's chagrin.

On the recommendation of a scout, Busch turned his attention to Tom Alston, a power-hitting first baseman for the San Diego Padres of the Pacific Coast League. "Long Tom," so named because he stood 6'5" and had a 78-inch wingspan, batted .297 with 23 home runs and 101 runs batted in during 1953. Busch became so enamored with Alston that he surrendered two players and $100,000 to acquire the slugger, and flew to Los Angeles to participate in the contract signing.

Alston broke the Cardinals' color barrier on April 13, 1954, batting sixth as the Redbirds' opening day first sacker. He struggled to hit big league pitching, though, and was returned to the minors before the All-Star break. The pressure of being the Cardinals' first black player, and of trying to live up to the expectations created by the high price paid to get him, weighed heavily on Alston. Plagued by constant fatigue and weakness, he was eventually diagnosed with Neurasthenia, a disorder that manifested itself with physical symptoms but couldn't be fully explained by any known medical condition. Alston didn't return in 1954 and appeared in only 25 more games over the next three seasons.

Given the unfortunate brevity of Alston's career, the Cardinals are proud to have his 1956 home uniform and one of his game-used bats. Alston likely wore this jersey (opposite page) on April 22, his only home appearance that season. This style is memorable; it is the only regular-season jersey to not feature the birds on the bat crest after 1928.

Following Alston's short tenure, management began building its team around promising African-American players such as Curt Flood, Bill White and Bob Gibson. Soon after, the Cardinals' roster also included Latin-American players Julian Javier, Julio Gotay and Ed Olivares. This diversity was a critical component in the club's success in the 1960s.

"I have been hoping that it would happen, hoping and waiting, and now it's a wonderful feeling to know the dream has come true."
– Tom Alston after signing his contract with the Cardinals

Tom Alston's game-worn home jersey from 1956 and one of his game-used bats from the same period.

Gold Glove Awards

The Rawlings Gold Glove Award® is presented annually to the best defensive players in baseball by the Rawlings Sporting Goods Company.

When a survey of teams revealed 83 percent of active professionals used Rawlings gloves, the St. Louis-based manufacturer decided to honor The Finest in the Field® with a special trophy recognizing players' fielding excellence. Since 1957, the award has been given to one player at each position in both leagues. Winners are determined by a vote of major league managers and coaches.

Rawlings revolutionized baseball glove design in the 1920s with help from a Cardinals hurler. Bill Doak is credited with the idea for improving the baseball glove by adding a multi-thong web between the first finger and thumb. The revolutionary "Bill Doak model"

— with its natural pocket — stayed in Rawlings' glove line until 1953. In the late 1950s, third baseman Ken Boyer was an early adopter of the Rawlings' Trap-Eze® six-finger model, which later was shortstop Ozzie Smith's mitt of choice. From Stan Musial to Yadier Molina, many Cardinals players have chosen Rawlings gloves to make their marks on the diamond.

The Redbirds have had a number of Rawlings Gold Glove Award recipients, including center fielder Curt Flood, who won seven straight; pitcher Bob Gibson, who claimed nine in a row; and shortstop Ozzie Smith, who reeled off a string of 13 consecutive trophies. In 2011, Rawlings established the Platinum Glove Award® to recognize the best overall defensive player in each league. Catcher Yadier Molina won the award three times in its first four years.

St. Louis Cardinals Rawlings Gold Glove Award Winners

1958 Ken Boyer-3B	1975 Ken Reitz-3B	2000 Jim Edmonds-OF, Mike Matheny-C
1959 Ken Boyer-3B	1978 Keith Hernandez-1B	2001 Jim Edmonds-OF, Fernando Vina-2B
1960 Bill White-1B, Ken Boyer-3B	1979 Keith Hernandez-1B	2002 Jim Edmonds-OF, Edgar Renteria-SS
1961 Bill White-1B, Ken Boyer-3B	1980 Keith Hernandez-1B, Ozzie Smith-SS	Scott Rolen-3B, Fernando Vina-2B
1962 Bobby Shantz-P, Bill White-1B	1981 Keith Hernandez-1B, Ozzie Smith-SS	2003 Jim Edmonds-OF, Mike Matheny-C
1963 Bobby Shantz-P, Bill White-1B,	1982 Keith Hernandez-1B, Ozzie Smith-SS	Edgar Renteria-SS, Scott Rolen-3B
Ken Boyer-3B, Curt Flood-OF	1983 Willie McGee-OF, Ozzie Smith-SS	2004 Jim Edmonds-OF, Mike Matheny-C,
1964 Bill White-1B, Curt Flood-OF	1984 Joaquin Andujar-P, Ozzie Smith-SS	Scott Rolen-3B
1965 Bob Gibson-P, Bill White-1B, Curt Flood-OF	1985 Willie McGee-OF, Ozzie Smith-SS	2005 Jim Edmonds-OF
1966 Bob Gibson-P, Curt Flood-OF	1986 Willie McGee-OF, Ozzie Smith-SS	2006 Albert Pujols-1B, Scott Rolen-3B
1967 Bob Gibson-P, Curt Flood-OF	1987 Terry Pendleton-3B, Ozzie Smith-SS	2008 Yadier Molina-C
1968 Bob Gibson-P, Dal Maxvill-SS, Curt Flood-OF	1988 Ozzie Smith-SS	2009 Yadier Molina-C, Adam Wainwright-P
1969 Bob Gibson-P, Curt Flood-OF	1989 Terry Pendleton-3B, Ozzie Smith-SS	2010 Yadier Molina-C, Albert Pujols-1B
1970 Bob Gibson-P	1990 Ozzie Smith-SS	2011 Yadier Molina-C*
1971 Bob Gibson-P	1991 Tom Pagnozzi-C, Ozzie Smith-SS	2012 Yadier Molina-C*
1972 Bob Gibson-P	1992 Tom Pagnozzi-C, Ozzie Smith-SS	2013 Yadier Molina-C, Adam Wainwright-P
1973 Bob Gibson-P	1994 Tom Pagnozzi-C	2014 Yadier Molina-C*

Platinum Glove Award established in 2011, given to the best defensive player of the year from each league.

> *"Hernandez may be the best defensive first baseman ever. He did things no first baseman ever did. As far as throwing and bunt coverage, he gave a new dimension to playing the position."* – Tim McCarver on five-time Cardinals Gold Glover Keith Hernandez

RAWLINGS
GOLD GLOVE
AWARD

1960

MAJOR LEAGUE
★All-Star★
FIELDING TEAM

FOR THE Professional PLAYER

Rawlings
MADE IN U.S.A.

19   **3B ~ KEN BOYER**
THE SPORTING NEWS   60
NATIONAL LEAGUE ALL ~ STAR FIELDING TEAM

Ken Boyer's 1960 Rawlings Gold Glove Award.

A well-scored card is an art form in itself, just as these cards are from the 1940s through the present that feature fantastic cover art celebrating the Cardinals. The Museum has over 300 historic scorecards in its collection.

Stan Musial's jersey from his final Cardinals game on September 29, 1963.

"The Man" Retires

When he was called up in late 1941, many folks didn't quite know how to pronounce his surname. But, thanks to his exploits at the plate and some frustrated Brooklyn fans who inspired his nickname, everyone eventually knew him as "The Man."

For 22 years, Stan Musial forged a career that placed him among the game's all-time greats. A 24-time All-Star and member of three world championship teams, he won three National League Most Valuable Player Awards and seven batting titles. His 3,630 hits were divided evenly between Sportsman's Park and the road, exemplifying a consistency few could approach. Though not appreciated as a power hitter, Musial's iconic corkscrew stance generated 475 home runs, including five in one double-header in 1954. When he retired in 1963, Musial held or shared more than two dozen National League records.

As great as he was on the field, "The Man" was much more than a ballplayer. He volunteered his time and resources to a variety of philanthropic efforts, both discreetly and by attending a myriad of banquets and public functions. Whether he was at a children's hospital, senior living facility or a state dinner, Musial would entertain everyone with stories, jokes and tunes on his trusty harmonica. And he always made sure everyone who wanted an autograph received one, even stocking the trunk of his car with pre-signed postcards to accommodate the large number of requests. He was buddies with the likes of John F. Kennedy and Pope John Paul II, yet the humble slugger frequently asked people who addressed him as "Mr. Musial" to simply call him "Stan."

Musial met every United States president from Harry Truman to Barack Obama, with the lone exception of Dwight Eisenhower. President Obama awarded Musial the United States' highest civilian honor in 2011, the Presidential Medal of Freedom. He stated during the ceremony that Stan was "an icon, untarnished, a beloved pillar of the community, a gentleman you would want your kids to emulate." The ceremony echoed an event held years earlier, when Musial received the Cavalier Cross of the Order of Merit, the highest civilian honor given by Poland, his father's homeland.

Musial remained active with the Cardinals, serving as an executive vice president and, in 1967, general manager. After his front-office stint, he became more involved in business interests, including a restaurant he co-owned and a sporting goods company that featured his name.

One of the most popular attractions in the Cardinals Hall of Fame and Museum is an area called "Holding History," where guests put on gloves and examine a bat used by one of six Cardinals greats. Musial's is far and away the most popular; simply holding his bat and making this connection with "The Man" has brought tears to the eyes of many.

"Take a look, fans. Take a good, long look. Remember the swing and the stance. We won't see his like again."
– Cardinals broadcaster Harry Caray during Musial's final big league at bat

Ken Boyer

Missouri native Ken Boyer was born into a family of 14 children. All seven Boyer boys grew up to play professional baseball and three of them — Ken, Cloyd and Clete — made it to major leagues.

On a scout's recommendation, the Cardinals held a special workout for Ken after his high school graduation. Though he was a skilled infielder and outfielder, the team signed him as a pitcher in 1949. Boyer's mound performance proved mediocre but he impressed whenever his manager plugged him in at third base. His agility in the field and his stroke at the plate convinced the front office that Boyer belonged in the everyday lineup. Two years of Army service briefly stalled his development,but after a strong 1954 campaign in Double-A, Boyer cracked the Cardinals roster in 1955.

While his rookie season was admirable, Boyer really clicked the following year, stroking 26 home runs with 98 runs batted in and a .306 average — earning his first of 11 National League All-Star nods. In 1957, the Redbirds moved the versatile Boyer to center field, opening third base for rookie Eddie Kasko. Boyer led all NL center fielders in fielding percentage that year but when the club traded for Curt Flood in 1958, Boyer shifted back to the hot corner and won his first of five Rawlings Gold Glove Awards.

Recognizing Boyer's leadership, the Cardinals named him team captain in August 1959, an uncommon move for the franchise. The 28-year-old responded by churning out six consecutive seasons with at least 24 home runs and 94 runs batted in. In 1964, he claimed the league's Most Valuable Player Award, leading the Senior Circuit with 119 runs batted in while batting .295 with 30 doubles.

Boyer started slowly in the 1964 World Series, banging just one hit during the first three games and watching his team fall behind two games to one. In the sixth inning of Game 4, though, he broke out with a grand slam, erasing a 3-0 New York Yankees lead and turning the Series around. In the deciding Game 7, Boyer added three more hits, including a solo home run. Ken's brother, Clete, answered with his own homer for the Yankees, making them the only brothers to homer in a Fall Classic game, but it wasn't enough to prevent the Cardinals' first world championship in 18 years.

Boyer was traded following the 1965 season but returned to the organization following his retirement to pursue a career in coaching. He managed the Cardinals from 1978-80 and was offered the managerial post at Triple-A in 1982 but a lung-cancer diagnosis forced him to the sidelines. Boyer died that September at age 52. His uniform No. 14 is the only one retired by the Cardinals for a player that is not in the National Baseball Hall of Fame.

"He was the boss of our field. He was the guy everyone looked up to."
– Tim McCarver, Cardinals catcher

Ken Boyer's game-worn home uniform from his rookie campaign in 1955; and a 1964 Cardinals Yearbook featuring the 1963 All-Star infield of Boyer, Dick Groat, Julian Javier and Bill White.

Rawlings
"Hall of Fame"
FLANNEL   44

Ken Boyer

1964 World Series

Knowing the legendary Stan Musial was playing his final season, the 1963 Cardinals had additional incentive to send "The Man" out a winner. A double-header sweep in mid-September cut a late-August, 7.5-game deficit down to a single game and hopes were high. Unfortunately, the club dropped eight of its final 10 games to wind up in second place.

With Musial no longer penciled into the lineup in 1964, fans didn't quite know what to expect from this

1964 World Series
press pin

new era of Cardinals baseball. The team played admirably during the first two months of the season and was just a game out of first on May 22. But a 6-17 stretch dropped the club into eighth place by June 15 — which happened to be the day General Manager Bing Devine made a trade that is still ranked among the greatest in baseball history. Devine sent pitcher Ernie Broglio and two others to the Chicago Cubs for outfielder Lou Brock and a pair of pitchers. The swap was unpopular at the time; few could envision how dramatically the move would change the team's fortunes.

The improvement didn't happen right away. Though the club climbed to fifth place by mid-August, it remained nine out — two games further off the pace then it stood the day of the Brock trade. So on August 18, owner Gussie Busch relieved Devine of his duties. Many of the players were not fond of the move but it did seem to light a fire under the team.

Led by National League Most Valuable Player Ken Boyer's 119 runs batted in, Bob Gibson's 19 wins and Brock's .348 average and 33 stolen bases, the Cardinals began closing the gap. The Redbirds overcame a 6.5-game deficit in the final 13 games to win the pennant on the final day of the season.

The momentum carried into the World Series against the New York Yankees, highlighted by Boyer's Game 4 grand slam and Tim McCarver's three-run shot to win Game 5. Bob Gibson held down the Bronx Bombers in the finale, earning his third win of the Series and another world championship for St. Louis.

In an ironic twist, Devine was honored as the 1964 Executive of the Year by The Sporting News, even though he had been out of the post since mid-August. Manager Johnny Keane, who was on the hot seat himself before the team made its historic run, shocked everyone by resigning the day after the Series ended. Three days later, he was introduced as the Yankees new manager.

Bill White's 1964 World Series ring

"We just wouldn't quit. It felt like we won every big game down the stretch when we had to." – Dick Groat, Cardinals shortstop

Lou Brock's 1964 game-worn road jersey; Dal Maxvill's 1964 home jersey, worn while catching the final out of the World Series; a Bill White game-used bat from the era; a souvenir pennant; and a hand-painted baseball given to Bob Howsam, Bing Devine's replacement, by owner Gussie Busch.

Red Schoendienst

With more championship rings than fingers, acquired during nearly 65 years of wearing the birds on the bat, this "Red" bird has embodied the essence of the Cardinals like few others in the history of the franchise.

Albert Fred Schoendienst was born in Germantown, Illinois, a small burg about 40 miles east of St. Louis, but didn't attend a Cardinals game until he was called up to play in one. Nicknamed "Red" for the carrot-colored crop under his cap, Schoendienst dropped out of school at age 16 and joined the Civilian Conversation Corp. While building fences one day, a nail ricocheted into his eye, nearly ending his baseball career before it ever began.

Fully recovered, the 19-year-old hitchhiked to a tryout camp at Sportsman's Park in 1942. Schoendienst made the first-day's cut and was asked to return for a second look. The club worked him out for a week before ultimately signing the switch-hitting infielder to a contract. Schoendienst ascended through the minors fairly quickly. He led the Triple-A International League with a .337 average in his third professional season, the youngest hitter to do so since 1892. Following a stint in the Army, he was ready for big league action.

When he arrived at spring training in 1945, there were no openings on the infield where he normally played, with regulars Whitey

Kurowski, Marty Marion and Emil Verban entrenched at third, short and second. The team did need a left fielder, though, since Stan Musial had just enlisted in the Navy. Schoendienst was installed as Musial's roster replacement and even adopted his uniform number 6. As a rookie, he batted .278 and led the league in stolen bases. When Musial returned the following season, Schoendienst moved to second base and switched to number 2, a digit that would later be retired in his honor. Red and Stan would lead the club to the 1946 world championship and become lifelong friends.

Schoendienst led the league in second base fielding percentage four times and was selected to nine All-Star teams as a Redbird. His dramatic home run in the 14th inning of the 1950 Midsummer Classic was a game-winner for the National League. Red was traded away in 1956 but returned to St. Louis in 1961 and retired in 1963. He ranks among the franchise's top 10 in games played, hits, runs, doubles and total bases.

In 1965, Schoendienst was hired to manage the Cardinals, embarking on a second calling that would prove to be as successful as his playing career. He led the team to the 1967 world championship and revisited the Fall Classic the following season. Schoendienst held the manager's post through 1976, returning for short stints in 1980 and 1990. His 1,041 wins are second-most in franchise history.

"Everything I have in my life I owe to baseball. I've been lucky in so many ways, making a career out of something I loved to do as a kid." – Red Schoendienst

Cardinals

Cardinals

2

Best Wishes
Red Schoendienst
5-10-46

Red Schoendienst
1968 Gamar

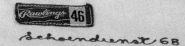
Rawlings 46
Schoendienst 68

Red Schoendienst's game-worn road jersey from 1946, his second season in the majors; and his home jersey from 1968, in which he led the Redbirds to a second consecutive pennant.

The baseball Mike Shannon hit for the first Cardinals home run at Civic Center Busch Memorial Stadium in 1966.

The Cardinals' New Nest

In the late 1950s, an exodus of businesses from downtown St. Louis had left the central city with many empty, outdated buildings and vacant lots. Four miles away, the Cardinals' home stadium had become equally obsolete and in need of replacement. City leaders believed a new downtown stadium — anchoring a larger urban renewal project —could solve both predicaments, and the Cardinals agreed.

The firm of Sverdrup & Parcel and Associates was hired as principal architects and engineers for the stadium, and world-renowned architect Edward Durrell Stone served as a design consultant. Stone used drawings of the soon-to-be-built Gateway Arch as inspiration for the 96 arches that would circle the ballpark's canopy. With financing for the 34-block downtown redevelopment in place, ground was broken for Civic Center Busch Memorial Stadium in May 1964.

On May 8, 1966, the arrival of a helicopter transporting home plate from the team's former grounds at Grand and Dodier — where the Redbirds played their first 10 home games that season — highlighted the dedication ceremony. Four days later, the Cardinals opened their new home with a come-from-behind, extra-inning win against the Atlanta Braves. Fittingly, a St. Louisan — Mike Shannon — hit the final Cardinals' home run at the old ballpark and the first Redbirds' blast in the new downtown stadium.

Busch was built as a multi-purpose facility, and its other primary tenant was the St. Louis Cardinals of the National Football League. The St. Louis Stars of the North American Soccer League had two stints as well. Numerous artists performed concerts there including The Beatles, Billy Joel, Elton John, Fleetwood Mac, the Rolling Stones, U2 and The Who. Many high school baseball and football games were hosted on the turf along with marching band competitions, tractor pulls, monster truck rallies and circuses.

The downtown stadium would host 3,227 Major League Baseball games over its 40 seasons. From Ray Washburn's first pitch in 1966 to Yadier Molina's last swing of the 2005 National League Championship Series, Busch Stadium saw its share of exciting, dramatic, disappointing and amazing moments. Among the highlights: Major League Baseball's All-Star Game in 1966; Bob Gibson's record 17-strikeout game in the 1968 World Series; Lou Brock's 3,000th-hit and then-season-record 105th stolen base; Bruce Sutter's strikeout of Gorman Thomas to end the 1982 World Series; Ozzie Smith's "Go crazy!" postseason long ball in 1985; Mark McGwire's historic 62nd and 70th home runs in 1998; and Jim Edmonds' game-saving, diving catch that helped send the Redbirds to the 2004 Fall Classic — one night after his walk-off home run kept the team's hopes alive.

"I have these memories here of this ballpark. The first night we played here, I had three base hits. I got the first Cardinal extra-base hit. The first Cardinal RBI. The first Cardinal home run. You can't take that away from me. It's in my mind. It's there forever." – Mike Shannon

St. Louis All-Star Games

Since 1933, the Major League Baseball All-Star Game has featured the game's top players in a battle for league supremacy. The first contest was intended to be a one-time event — created to complement the World's Fair in Chicago — but it proved so popular that Commissioner Kenesaw Mountain Landis decreed immediately that it become an annual affair.

The exhibition has been played every year at the midpoint of the season in ballparks selected by Major League Baseball, with one exception in 1945 due to wartime travel restrictions. In 1959, the leagues began holding two All-Star Games each year but abandoned the practice after 1962.

A variety of methods have been employed through the years to select players for each team. The current practice of allowing fans to vote for the eight starting position players was adopted in 1970. Since 2003, home-field advantage in the World Series has been awarded to the team whose league won the Midsummer Classic, adding an extra twist to the competition.

Sportsman's Park/Busch Stadium 1 hosted the All-Star Game three times. In its debut season, Busch Memorial Stadium was the site of the 1966 contest, played on a day when the temperature reached 105 degrees in St. Louis. It took 43 years for the All-Stars to return to the Gateway City, with the most recent game being played at the current Busch Stadium in 2009.

All-Star Games in St. Louis

Year	Host	Location	Result
1940	Cardinals	Sportsman's Park	NL 4, AL 0
1948	Browns	Sportsman's Park	AL 5, NL 2
1957	Cardinals	Busch Stadium (1953-66)	AL 6, NL 5
1966	Cardinals	Busch Memorial Stadium	NL 2, AL 1
2009	Cardinals	Busch Stadium (2006-Present)	AL 4, NL 3

In 2009, President Barack Obama threw the ceremonial first pitch at the All-Star Game. He was the first U.S. leader to do so since Gerald Ford in 1976, and only the fourth Commander in Chief to take the hill in the exhibition's history.

"Hosting the All-Star Game here in the place that you play with the fans and everybody, and a special presence by the president showing up and throwing the first pitch... probably, it will be the best All-Star Game that I'm ever going to have." – Albert Pujols on the 2009 All-Star Game

One of Stan Musial's specially marked game-used bats from the 1957 All-Star Game in St. Louis; a 2009 All-Star Game baseball autographed by Stan Musial and Albert Pujols; press pins from the games held in 1948, 1957, 1966 and 2009; and the 1940 All-Star Game program.

PROGRAM ★

LOUISVILLE SLUGGER
125
RICH & BRADSBY CO
MADE IN U.S.A.
LOUISVILLE KY.

Powerized

ALL STAR GAME
MUSIAL MODEL
ST. LOUIS 1957

MAJOR LEAGUE
ALL STAR
GAME

TUESDAY
JULY 9,
1940
1:30 P.M.

SPORTSMANS
PARK
SAINT
LOUIS

Price 25 Cents

1957
ALL STAR
PRESS

ALL-STAR GAME
ST. LOUIS
1948

All-Star Game
2009

1966
ALL STAR
GAME
ST. LOUIS

1967 World Series

In the wake of the 1964 club's incredible run to the crown, fans were hopeful they wouldn't need to wait 18 years — as they just had — for a repeat title. But seventh and sixth place finishes the next two seasons made another pennant chase seem like a distant hope.

General Manager Bob Howsam began remaking the roster after the 1965 season, trading away cornerstone players Ken Boyer and Bill White. The shrewd acquisitions of Orlando Cepeda in May 1966 and Roger Maris that December supplemented a nucleus that still included productive stars Lou Brock, Curt Flood, Bob Gibson and a young Steve Carlton. Howsam didn't stick around to see his project through, though, departing for Cincinnati in January 1967. Owner Gussie Busch installed Stan Musial to replace Howsam.

The new-look Redbirds emerged from the gate quickly, winning seven of their first eight games. Brock batted .400 in April at the top of the order and cleanup hitter Cepeda established a sizzling pace he would carry throughout the season — resulting in his choice as National League Most Vauable Player. Cepeda also brought an energized vibe to the clubhouse, blasting salsa music

1967 World Series press pin

and nurturing a decidedly Latin American atmosphere. "Cha Cha" christened his team "El Birdos," a moniker that gained popularity among Cardinals fans.

Just as the offense had turned the page, so too did the pitching staff. Among the club's six main starters, five had earned run averages of 3.01 or less. Gibson, the staff ace, was struck by a Roberto Clemente line drive July 15 and suffered a broken leg, putting him on the shelf until September 7. When he returned, the Redbirds held an 11.5-game lead and already had the pennant within their grasp.

Their Fall Classic opponents would be American League Triple Crown winner Carl Yastrzemski and his Boston Red Sox. The teams split the first six games, with Boston winning Games 5 and 6 to force a winner-take-all bout at Fenway Park. The Cardinals tabbed Gibson to take the mound while the Sox countered with 22-game winner Jim Lonborg. Each ace had already recorded two wins in the Series and was pitching on short rest. The headline in Boston's newspaper that morning read, "LONBORG AND CHAMPAGNE" but it was Gibson who prevailed, surrendering only two hits in a 7-2 triumph.

The Champagne ended up in the visitors' clubhouse, as did the first permanent trophy presented to the World Series champion by Major League Baseball. Officially called "The Commissioner's Trophy" (as of 1985), the inaugural award is proudly preserved in the Cardinals Museum collection.

Stan Musial's
1967 Cardinals
World Series ring

"What a special relationship the players on that team and the fans had. And the character of the club, the camaraderie of that club, the blended talent, is something that a lot of teams never capture." – Nelson Briles, Cardinals pitcher

Game-worn 1967 home and road jerseys from Orlando Cepeda and Steve Carlton; game-used bats from Cepeda and Brock; souvenirs from the 1967 season; and the very first World Series championship trophy.

Bob Gibson

He retired as the greatest pitcher in Cardinals history but Bob Gibson's dominance on the Major League diamond wasn't immediately evident.

Born shortly after the death of his father, Gibson looked to his older brother, Josh, to be a mentor, father figure and role model. Creighton-educated Josh was a recreation center director who organized sports teams for Omaha-area youth, including Bob. The little brother's athleticism was never in doubt; Gibson excelled at baseball, track and field events, and his favorite activity, basketball. The Cardinals offered him a nominal contract out of high school but Gibson opted to pursue college hoops, ultimately landing at Josh's alma mater where he became the first African-American to play basketball there. Gibson also played baseball at Creighton and attracted interest from several professional teams in both sports.

In the spring of 1957, Gibson was courted by the Harlem Globetrotters, the world-famous, barnstorming basketball team. When the school year ended, Gibson chose to sign with the Cardinals for the rest of the season, after which he would fulfill a four-month contract with the Globetrotters — and then renegotiate with St. Louis. The Redbirds saw enough raw ability in the powerful right hander to know they wanted him to focus on baseball. The club offered an additional $4,000 during contract talks as incentive to give up basketball. It worked.

Gibson was called up to the majors to start the 1959 campaign but shuttled back and forth between St. Louis and Triple-A until he stuck with the Cardinals for good in 1961. During these early years, Gibby struggled with his control and sometimes with his manager. He showed flashes of brilliance but after the 1961 season, Gibson owned a mediocre 19-23 career record and 3.80 earned run average.

Things began to click in 1962, though, as Gibson led the league with five shutouts and made his first All-Star team. During the next decade, Gibson won 189 of the 332 games he started, throwing 203 complete games — 46 of them shutouts — and averaging 273 innings pitched per season. In 1968, he registered arguably the most impressive season by a major league pitcher during the live-ball era. In his $304^{2/3}$ innings pitched, Gibby allowed just 38 earned-runs for a modern-era earned-run average record of 1.12. He tossed 28 complete games, 13 shutouts, and struck out 268 batters while walking just 62. The intimidating right hander saved his best game for the World Series, fanning 17 hitters in defeating 31-game-winner Denny McLain and the Detroit Tigers in the Series opener.

Gibson retired as the franchise leader in wins, complete games, shutouts, innings pitched and strikeouts. He and Stan Musial are the only Cardinals with retired numbers who exclusively wore the birds on the bat.

"He had to be the hardest pitcher I ever caught, with that fastball moving and sailing away like a belligerent butterfly."
– Tim McCarver, Cardinals catcher

Bob Gibson's 1969 Rawlings Gold Glove Award, one of nine he won during his career; his 1968 game-worn home jersey; and his 1968 National League Cy Young Award.

MATT HOLLIDAY

RED SCHOENDIENST

ROLEN

MARK McGWIRE

Bobbleheads didn't become a popular souvenir until the mid-1960s; however fans' interest in them has exploded in the past few decades. The Museum collection houses well over 100 different nodders, who constantly agree that more are needed.

A pair of Lou Brock's game-worn cleats from the 1960s; Brock's Jun Ishii-model bat, used for his 3,000th-hit; and his game-worn road jersey from 1974.

Lou Brock

In baseball, memorable steals typically take place on the field, between first and second base or, occasionally, when a runner breaks for home. But the game's greatest heist may have occurred between two organizations — and not in a boardroom or an executive office, but a phone booth.

Cardinals General Manager Bing Devine knew his job was on the line in June 1964 after a weekend sweep in Los Angeles dropped the team below .500. With the trade deadline imminent, Devine explored some potential deals before flying to Houston. One of his first calls was made to Chicago Cubs GM John Holland; Chicago needed pitching and the Cardinals wanted help in the outfield. Devine and Holland had discussed certain players weeks earlier — including speedy outfielder Lou Brock — but were unable to consummate a deal. This time, when Devine inquired about Brock, Holland responded that the Cubs were ready to act — but wanted former 20-game winner Ernie Broglio in return. Four other players were attached to the deal to balance out each team's positional needs.

Before finalizing the trade, Devine wanted to run it past manager Johnny Keane. He boarded the charter flight, leaned over to his manager and said, "Looks like we could make a deal where the key players are Brock and Broglio." Keane simply responded, "What are we waiting for?" Devine found a pay phone as soon as the plane landed and made the move.

The trade was panned initially by players and fans alike. Broglio had won 18 games the year before and boasted a 70-55 career record, all with the Cardinals.

Brock was a project with a career batting average below .260, a result of being pressured to hit for power. During their first meeting, Keane told Brock to forget about the long ball and focus on getting on base — and once there, to run any time he wanted. An energized Brock batted .348 with 33 stolen bases the rest of the year for the Cardinals, which went 65-38 after the trade and overcame a 6.5-game deficit the final two weeks of the season to vault into the World Series.

Brock continued getting on base regularly the next 15 seasons, recording his 3,000th career hit against his former club on August 13, 1979. He also never stopped running, swiping 888 of his then-record 938 stolen bases for the Cardinals. However, Brock came up biggest when the spotlight was brightest. He was a force in the Fall Classic, batting .391 in 21 World Series games with 16 runs scored, 14 stolen bases and 13 runs batted in. He still holds the record for stolen bases in a single World Series, with seven.

In Cardinals history, Brock ranks first in stolen bases and leadoff home runs; second in hits, games played, runs and at-bats; third in doubles and total bases; fourth in triples; sixth in walks; and ninth in runs batted in.

"If there are any lobsters left in Boston, Lou Brock will go back and get them. He's stolen everything else in the town."
– Red Schoendienst, Cardinals manager, after Brock set a World Series stolen base record in 1967

No-Hitters

Few accomplishments in sports hold the appeal of a no-hitter. One can occur on any night, in any ballpark, against any team. It's never anticipated — at least not until the seventh inning or so, when most realize it's happening. One game. Twenty-seven outs. No hits. Baseball immortality.

The St. Louis Cardinals trace their statistical history back to 1892, the first year of the franchise's continuous membership in the National League. Since then, eight different Redbird pitchers have tossed nine no-hitters.

Jesse Haines is credited with the team's first no-no, blanking the Boston Braves in 1924. A decade later, Paul Dean crafted the club's next hitless gem during the second game of a double-header. Brother Dizzy, who had carried a no-hitter through eight innings of the day's first game—before surrendering three hits in the ninth—told Paul afterward, "If I'd a-known you was gonna throw a no-hitter, I'd a-throw'ed one too!"

Lon Warneke faced just 28 batters — one over the minimum — in his 1941 no-hitter. Two infield errors were erased by double plays, but Warneke's lone walk in the seventh inning resulted in a stranded runner.

The Cardinals were part of a major league first in September 1968. One day after San Francisco Giants hurler Gaylord Perry no-hit the El Birdos, Redbird righty Ray Washburn returned the favor. It marked the first time that teams had traded no-hitters on consecutive days.

Bob Gibson put an exclamation point on one of the greatest pitching careers ever with a no-hitter in 1971, shutting down the eventual World Series champion Pittsburgh Pirates in their own ballpark.

The only Cardinal to throw multiple no-hitters — and the only hurler to toss a no-no at Busch Memorial Stadium — was Bob Forsch. His first came on a cold April day in 1978, while the second happened five years later.

It would be 16 years until the next Cardinals no-hitter, in which Jose Jimenez outdueled future Hall of Famer Randy Johnson. Two years later, Bud Smith became the second Redbird rookie, along with Paul Dean, to leave his opponent hitless.

St. Louis Cardinals No-Hitters

Date	Pitcher	Opponent	Score	Date	Pitcher	Opponent	Score
July 17, 1924	Jesse Haines	Boston Braves	5-0	April 16, 1978	Bob Forsch	Philadelphia Phillies	5-0
September 21, 1934	Paul Dean	At Brooklyn Dodgers	3-0	September 26, 1983	Bob Forsch	Montreal Expos	3-0
August 30, 1941	Lon Warneke	At Cincinnati Reds	2-0	June 25, 1999	Jose Jimenez	At Arizona Diamondbacks	1-0
September 18, 1968	Ray Washburn	At San Francisco Giants	2-0	September 3, 2001	Bud Smith	At San Diego Padres	4-0
August 14, 1971	Bob Gibson	At Pittsburgh Pirates	11-0				

"I've had a pretty bad season, but at least I salvaged something. To throw one is something, but two is a fantastic thing."
– Bob Forsch after his second no-hitter

Scorecards from Jesse Haines' no-hitter in 1924 and Bob Gibson's gem in 1971; the pitching rubber from Jose Jimenez' no-no in 1999; the trophy presented to Paul Dean in 1934 for his no-hit performance; pitching coach Dave Duncan's pitch chart from Bud Smith's no-hit affair in 2001; and Bob Forsch's trophy balls from his no-hitters in 1978 and 1983.

Whitey Herzog

Throughout the 1970s, Cardinals fans experienced great individual performances that included Joe Torre's MVP campaign, Bob Gibson's no-hitter, Lou Brock's stolen-base heroics and Ted Simmons' consistent slugging. Unfortunately they didn't see any championships. Nobody was more annoyed by the dry spell than owner Gussie Busch, who fired three managers in five seasons.

After a slow start in 1980, Busch and his staff focused on the one candidate they believed could change the club's fortunes. His name was Dorrel Norman Elvert Herzog, but everyone called him "Whitey." The New Athens, Illinois, native and former Kansas City Royals manager rejected an offer to come on board as a consultant, then turned down a one-year contract to become manager because he had tired of short-term deals in Kansas City. Herzog told Busch, "I want some hammer," and Gussie complied with a three-year agreement.

Herzog debuted in the Cardinals dugout June 9 and soon decided the Redbirds' issues ran much deeper than their inability to execute on the field. In his opinion, a radical clubhouse cleansing was needed. Whitey took his concerns straight to the top, telling Busch, "If I had known it was this bad, maybe I wouldn't have come." Busch loved Whitey's honesty, and agreed to Herzog's request to step out of his cleats and into the general manager's shoes. Whitey wasted little time remaking the roster, trading 14 players,

signing six and releasing two before the start of the 1981 season. With the team he wanted in place, Herzog returned to the dugout.

The roster turnover worked magnificently. The Cardinals finished 1981 with the best overall record in the National League Eastern division, however, they didn't make the playoffs because a players' strike split the season into two halves — and the Redbirds didn't win either one. Herzog liked his club, but felt a slick-fielding shortstop, like San Diego's Ozzie Smith, could be the final piece to his puzzle. Smith, who had a no-trade clause, agreed to relocate to St. Louis after Herzog told him, "If you come and play for us, there's no reason we can't go and win it all."

With a team built around speed and defense that was well-suited to Busch Stadium's distant fences and artificial turf — Herzog had created an exciting style of baseball that came to be known as "Whitey Ball." Herzog's club won the world championship in 1982 and returned to the Fall Classic in 1985 and 1987.

Herzog was beloved in St. Louis not only because his teams won but also because Cardinals fans connected with his down-home, honest approach toward baseball, beer and life in general. Those same traits endeared him to Busch, who thanks to Herzog, was able to again savor winning baseball before his death in 1989. Herzog was the Cardinals' second-winningest manager when he left the club in 1990.

"He's the guy I've been looking for 29 years. He's not only a great manager, but a helluva guy. He and I talk the same language." – Gussie Busch, Cardinals owner

Whitey Herzog's 1981 "victory blue" game-worn road jersey; and team-signed baseballs from each of his three Cardinals World Series appearances.

125
Louisville Slugger®
Louisville, Kentucky Made in U.S.A.

HILLERICH & BRADSBY CO.

SILVER SLUGGER ℠
AWARD

PRESENTED TO

BOB FORSCH - P

ST. LOUIS

MEMBER OF THE SPORTING NEWS
NATIONAL LEAGUE OFFENSIVE TEAM

1980

TED SIMMONS-C	MIKE SCHMIDT-3B
KEITH HERNANDEZ-1B	DUSTY BAKER-OF
MANNY TRILLO-2B	ANDRE DAWSON-OF
GARRY TEMPLETON-SS	GEORGE HENDRICK-OF

Silver Slugger Winners

The Silver Slugger℠ Awards are given annually to the best offensive players in baseball by Hillerich & Bradsby, maker of Louisville Slugger® bats. Hillerich & Bradsby has been in the bat business since 1884, almost as long as professional baseball has existed.

Until recent years, nearly every notable Cardinals hitter used Louisville Sluggers at one point or another. Three Louisville Slugger bat finishes — Hornsby, Walker and Van Slyke — are even named for former Redbirds Rogers, Harry and Andy; and the cupped end popular among many of today's players can be traced to Lou Brock, who requested the modification after being introduced to similar bats during a tour of Japan.

The iconic, Kentucky-based company began awarding the Silver Slugger Awards in 1980 as an extension of its Silver Bat Award, a trophy it presented to the batting champion in each league. The Silver Sluggers are voted on by coaches and managers, and presented to the top hitters at each position. Voters consider a number of factors and statistics, including batting average, on-base percentage and slugging percentage.

The Cardinals have had a number of Silver Slugger recipients, including Albert Pujols, who captured six; Edgar Renteria, who claimed three; and Bob Forsch, who won two as a pitcher. The Cardinals Museum is proud to have both of Forsch's awards in its collection. The 1980 award features five Redbird Silver Sluggers.

St. Louis Cardinals Silver Slugger Award Winners

Date	Player	Position	Date	Player	Position	Date	Player	Position
1980	Bob Forsch	Pitcher	1998	Mark McGwire	First Base	2005	Jason Marquis	Pitcher
	George Hendrick	Outfield	2000	Edgar Renteria	Shortstop	2008	Ryan Ludwick	Outfield
	Keith Hernandez	First Base	2001	Albert Pujols	Third Base		Albert Pujols	First Base
	Ted Simmons	Catcher	2002	Edgar Renteria	Shortstop	2009	Albert Pujols	First Base
	Garry Templeton	Shortstop		Scott Rolen	Third Base	2010	Matt Holliday	Outfield
1983	George Hendrick	First Base	2003	Albert Pujols	Outfield		Albert Pujols	First Base
1985	Jack Clark	First Base		Edgar Renteria	Shortstop	2013	Yadier Molina	Catcher
	Willie McGee	Outfield	2004	Jim Edmonds	Outfield		Matt Carpenter	Second Base
1987	Jack Clark	First Base		Albert Pujols	First Base			
	Bob Forsch	Pitcher						
	Ozzie Smith	Shortstop						

"I was proud because it was a goal I had set for myself and had achieved. I knew it would make people more aware that I was a better offensive player than I had been given credit for."
– Ozzie Smith, on batting .303 with 75 runs batted in during his 1987 Silver Slugger Award-winning season

A presentational home plate — illustrated by noted sports cartoonist Amadee Wohlschlaeger and signed by the 1982 Cardinals — that was given to Glenn Brummer to commemorate his daring theft.

Brummer Steals Home

The Cardinals had high expectations going into 1982 after posting the best record in their division during the strike-shortened 1981 season. An early 12-game winning streak fed the excitement but the team played uninspired baseball throughout the summer and trailed Philadelphia by three games in August. They needed a spark; nobody could anticipate it would come from a third-string catcher.

On August 22, the Redbirds had regained a slim lead in the division and just split the first two games of a weekend series against the San Francisco Giants. With Joaquin Andujar on the mound in the rubber game, the Cardinals jumped out to a 3-0 lead. The Giants put four on the board in the sixth before a run-scoring double by Ken Oberkfell in the bottom of the ninth sent the game into extra frames. Both teams threatened in the 10th and 11th innings, but neither could deliver the key hit.

That's when Glenn Brummer decided to take matters into his own hands. Brummer had entered the game in the bottom of the eighth as a pinch runner and stayed in to catch. With one out in the 12th inning, he singled off Gary Lavelle, the Giants' lanky left-hander. He advanced to second on a Willie McGee single before an infield hit by Ozzie Smith loaded the bases for David Green.

Perched 90 feet from victory, Brummer noticed that Lavelle had a high leg kick, was slow to home and was pitching out of the stretch. He also felt the pitcher wasn't paying attention to the slow-footed catcher at third. With each pitch, Brummer tested his walking lead another step or so before retreating to the bag. After Green ran the count to 2-1, Brummer looked at third base coach Chuck Hiller and said, "You know, I can go. Should I?" Hiller responded, "Better not." As much as Brummer wanted to run on the 2-1 pitch, he obeyed his coach and watched Green take strike two.

Brummer didn't ask for advice or permission before the next pitch. As soon as Lavelle went into his delivery, Brummer began barreling home. Seeing the runner advancing in his peripheral vision, catcher Milt May leaped from his crouch, lunged forward and planted his left shin guard on the outside edge of the plate. Brummer's outstretched hand swept across home a split second before the pitch hit May's mitt, ending the game in the most unexpected way possible.

To this day, some fans and sportswriters believe the pitch should have been called a strike, which would have ended the inning and kept the game alive. Others suggest the game was over the moment Brummer's fingers touched the plate, making the pitch's location irrelevant. The only opinion that truly mattered was home plate umpire Dave Pallone's. Brummer stole home and a place in Cardinals history.

"Brummer's stealing home! He is saaafe, and the Cardinals win! Brummer stole home! The dugout comes out and they congratulate him. You wouldn't believe it!"
– Mike Shannon's call on KMOX

1982 World Series

1982 World Series
press pin

It was the dawn of a new era in Cardinals baseball. Less than two years after Whitey Herzog had joined the organization, the club came to spring training in 1982 poised for a breakout season.

Fans were still adjusting to the new style of play that Herzog employed. The skipper transformed the club he inherited into a team that relied on speed, defense and pitching. The long ball was not a priority; Herzog preferred an up-tempo brand of "small ball" that became so ubiquitous with the Cardinals and their golden-haired manager that it was labeled "Whitey Ball."

Herzog had shaken up the roster dramatically in his short tenure, but felt some fine tuning was still needed. In October 1981, a seemingly minor deal at the time with the New York Yankees landed center fielder Willie McGee. Soon after, a three-team swap brought left fielder Lonnie Smith into the fold. Herzog's boldest move of the winter came two weeks before Christmas when shortstop Ozzie Smith was acquired from San Diego.

After a hot start, the team played mediocre baseball most of the season but still hovered near the top of their division. The Redbirds never trailed first place by more than three games

Stan Musial's 1982 Cardinals World Series ring

and never led by more than $6^{1/2}$, a high-water mark reached September 27 before losing four of their final five contests. Not surprisingly, the club led the National League in stolen bases, on-base percentage and triples — but finished last with just 67 home runs.

Brushing away a meaningless final week of the season, the Cardinals swept the Atlanta Braves in the franchise's first-ever National League Championship Series and faced off against the Milwaukee Brewers in the Fall Classic. Nicknamed "The Suds Series" because of the cities' brewery connections, the duel offered a unique match-up between the fleet-footed Redbirds and the heavy-hitting Brewers, whose 216 home runs easily led their league.

Milwaukee's bats dominated the opening game, winning 10-0 behind a 17-hit attack. The Cardinals bounced back from the drubbing with consecutive wins. In Game 3, McGee introduced himself to the national stage with two home runs and a pair of outstanding catches. The Brewers responded with dual victories of their own and returned to St. Louis one win from the title. With their backs against the wall, the Redbirds dished out a convincing 13-1 pounding in Game 6 that featured a clutch, four-hit complete game from rookie John Stuper. In the deciding game, after trailing 3-1 in the sixth inning, the Cardinals scored five unanswered runs to secure the Series.

"When you look at our team, nobody put fear in anybody at all. Nobody was afraid of us. They didn't even know they had been dominated until they got beat three times in a row and left."
– Darrell Porter, 1982 World Series MVP

The 1982 world championship trophy; Willie McGee's 1997 game-worn throwback jersey, celebrating the 1982 Series in which he also participated; a one-of-a-kind Rawlings glove crafted for August A. Busch Jr., commemorating the 1982 title; a 1982 team-signed baseball; Darrell Porter's game-worn cleats; and Bob Forsch's team-signed 1982 World Series bat.

Bruce Sutter

Most hurlers need to possess a wide arsenal of pitches to find success in the big leagues. Not Bruce Sutter. The bearded righty proved it's possible to ride a single pitch all the way to Cooperstown.

Two games into his professional career in the Chicago Cubs minor league system, Sutter was sidelined by a pinched nerve that required surgery. The following spring, he realized he no longer had a fastball. Fred Martin, a Cubs pitching instructor who previously spent parts of three seasons playing for the Cardinals, taught Sutter an unusual pitch to help him salvage his career — the split-fingered fastball. It took Sutter a few years to master the new offering, but the Cubs were patient. He made his Major League debut May 9, 1976 — throwing a scoreless frame in a blowout loss

— and recorded his first big league save three weeks later.

Sutter nailed down 37 saves in 1979 and won the National League Cy Young Award. His future looked bright in Chicago, but just one season later, he was shipped to St. Louis in exchange for three infielders. New manager Whitey Herzog had long coveted the elite reliever and finally got his guy after a year of negotiating with the Cubs front office.

The new addition performed as expected in 1981, establishing a Cardinals single-season record with 25 saves. He bested that mark in 1982, closing out 36 victories. Then in 1984, Sutter tied the major league record and set the National League standard with 45 saves. But the most unforgetable achievement that year was undoubtedly the moment he thrust his right fist into the air after striking out Gorman Thomas in the bottom of the ninth inning of Game 7 to close out the 1982 World Series championship.

Sutter pitched just four seasons for the Cardinals, but in three of those campaigns, he placed among the top five in Cy Young Award voting and top eight in Most Valuable Player Award balloting. That level of recognition is rare for relief pitchers of any earned run average, but was apropos for a hurler who won or saved almost half of his team's victories during his tenure in St. Louis. By current standards, Sutter's durability also was extraordinary. He pitched more than one inning in two-thirds of his relief appearances with the Cardinals and earned 15 saves when entering the game in the seventh inning.

Sutter retired with an even 300 saves, the third closer to reach that milestone. His 127 saves with the Redbirds still ranks among the top five in franchise history. The two-time Cardinals All-Star captured three Rolaids Relief Man Awards while wearing the birds on the bat. Sutter was the first pitcher inducted into the National Baseball Hall of Fame who never started a game.

"He had the best makeup of any closer I've ever seen. He just cut the percentages down for me from 27 outs a game to 21."
– Whitey Herzog, Cardinals manager

Bruce Sutter's 1982 game-worn road jersey; two of his baseball cards from the early 1980s; and a stadium give-away bobblehead from 2012.

8 FRANK FRISCH
St. Louis N. L.

ROBINSON, S.S., St. Louis
OLD JUDGE
CIGARETTE FACTORY.
GOODWIN & CO., New York.

BRESNAHAN St. Louis Nat'L

CARDINALS
Louis Evans
OF THE
ST. LOUIS NATIONALS

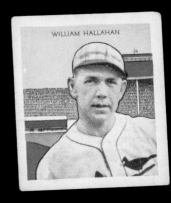

WILLIAM HALLAHAN

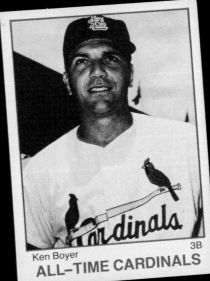

Ken Boyer   3B
ALL–TIME CARDINALS

GEORGE KUROWSKI
Third Base, St. Louis, N.L.

Ken O'Dea
1942-1946   St. Louis Cardinals   Catcher

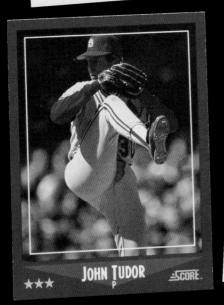

JOHN TUDOR
P
★★★   SCORE

Joe Magrane

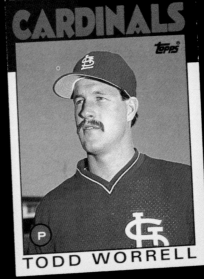

CARDINALS
TODD WORRELL

ALL Star   SS
NATIONAL LEAGUE
OZZIE SMITH

A popular collectible amongst generations of fans, the Cardinals maintain a collection of over 3,000 baseball cards, including a team set from the 1886 Old Judge Cigarette collection—one of the earliest-known offerings.

HORNSBY, ST. LOUIS NAT.

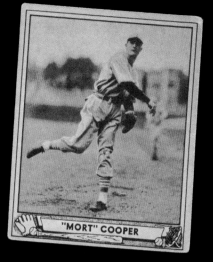

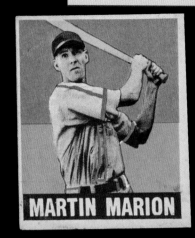

"MORT" COOPER

MARTIN MARION

Von McDaniel

PITCHER   ST. LOUIS CARDINALS

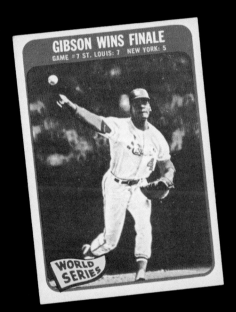

GIBSON WINS FINALE
GAME 7 ST. LOUIS: 7   NEW YORK: 5

WORLD SERIES

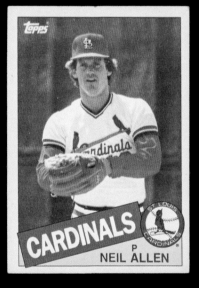

Topps

CARDINALS

P
NEIL ALLEN

KEN REITZ   3RD BASE

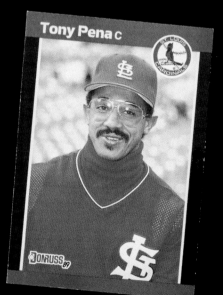

Tony Pena c

Donruss 89

PAGNOZZI
39

Pagnozzi • 1995

St. Louis Cardinals

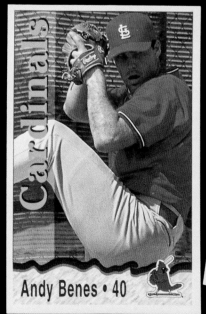

Cardinals

Andy Benes • 40

MVP

MORRIS
35

Rookies of the Year

The Rookie of the Year Award is given annually to the top freshman in each league, as voted on by the Baseball Writers Association of America. The inaugural Award was won by Jackie Robinson in 1947; four decades later, the plaque was renamed in his honor. The Cardinals have had six newcomers claim Rookie of the Year honors, and on two occasions they had players win the award in back-to-back seasons.

Wally Moon received the first Rookie of the Year Award in franchise history in 1954, gathering more votes than future Hall of Famers Ernie Banks and Henry Aaron. Moon batted .304 and finished the season among the league's top 10 in hits, runs, triples and at-bats. The following season teammate Bill Virdon slugged 17 long balls and 18 two-baggers to bring a second rookie title to St. Louis.

Almost 20 years elapsed before outfielder Bake McBride captured his Rookie of the Year honor. Flashing both leather and lumber, McBride ranked fourth among National League center fielders in fielding percentage and finished eighth in singles and batting average. He also stole 30 bases for good measure.

Another speedster, Vince Coleman, ran his way to Rookie of the Year recognition in 1985, swiping a first-year record 110 stolen bases while helping his club win the National League pennant. Coleman's rookie honor was matched in 1986 by reliever Todd Worrell who set a freshman record of his own at the time, collecting 36 saves with a 2.08 earned run average.

Albert Pujols burst onto the scene in 2001 with a season for the ages, winning the award in unanimous fashion — the first Cardinals player to do so. Pujols established a National League rookie mark with 130 runs batted in and set a franchise record for first-year players with 37 round-trippers. He finished the season among the league's top 10 in batting average, slugging percentage, hits, doubles and total bases.

St. Louis Cardinals Rookie of the Year Award Winners

1954	Wally Moon	Outfield
1955	Bill Virdon	Outfield
1974	Bake McBride	Outfield
1985	Vince Coleman	Outfield
1986	Todd Worrell	Pitcher
2001	Albert Pujols	Third Base/Outfield

"That man just took off. He absolutely ran away with the award. He really showed what can be done with speed, power and adaptability."
– Jimmy Rollins, Philadelphia Phillies All-Star shortstop, on 2001 Rookie of the Year Albert Pujols

Game-used, autographed bats from Cardinals Rookie of the Year Award winners: Wally Moon, Bill Virdon, Bake McBride, Vince Coleman, Todd Worrell and Albert Pujols.

Ozzie Smith

Most people experience a few moments in life when they can later recall exactly where they were and what they were doing. For many Cardinals fans, one of those extraordinary occasions happened October 14, 1985, during Game 5 of the National League Championship Series. That's when a five-foot-nine, 150-pound shortstop stepped to the left side of the plate in the bottom of the ninth inning with the score tied. A message flashed across the stadium scoreboard noting the switch-hitter had never hit a home run while batting left handed as a major leaguer. Four pitches later, Hall of Fame broadcaster Jack Buck — in a flash of inspired exuberance — told his listeners to "Go crazy, folks! Go crazy!"

To many, that autumn long ball is the most memorable moment of Ozzie Smith's Cardinals career. But it was his defense that defined his stardom and wowed legions of fans on a daily basis. Widely regarded as the finest-fielding shortstop of all time, "The Wizard" made extraordinary plays seem routine. Smith led the National League in fielding percentage seven times and is the major leagues' career leader in assists and total chances for shortstops. He won 11 straight Rawlings Gold Glove Awards as a Cardinal and was elected by baseball fans as the shortstop on the All-Time Rawlings Gold Glove team in 2007.

Fittingly, Smith used a Rawlings glove throughout his entire career. As a youngster, he was partial to the six-finger Trap-Eze® model, a design that didn't have mass-market appeal and eventually was discontinued. Once he became a pro, Smith convinced Rawlings to resurrect the pattern. It remains a popular item in the company's product line, primarily because it was favored by Ozzie.

Originally labeled as a "good-glove, no-hit" talent, Smith worked hard on his batting and developed into a legitimate offensive threat. Ozzie's most productive campaign came in 1987 when he batted .303 with 40 doubles, 104 runs, 89 walks, 75 runs batted in and an on-base percentage of .392. He placed second in the league's Most Valuable Player Award voting that season.

Each Opening Day, and occasionally in the playoffs, everyone knew it was time for Cardinals baseball when Smith bolted onto the turf and performed his signature back flip. A fan favorite in St. Louis and throughout the country, he was selected to 15 All-Star Games and, at the time of his retirement, had received more fan votes for the Midsummer Classic than any player in National League history. In 1982, The Wizard led the Cardinals to their first World Series championship in 15 years and returned to the Series two more times during the next five seasons. On the Cardinals all-time lists, Smith ranks in the top 10 in games played, at-bats, stolen bases, runs, hits, walks and doubles.

"I think of myself as an artist on the field. Every game I look for a chance to do something that the fans have never seen before." – Ozzie Smith

Ozzie Smith's 1992 game-worn home jersey, featuring the club's centennial anniversary patch; one of his game-used gloves from the early 1990s; and a game-used bat from the same era.

70 Home Runs

In the summer of 1998, a heated home run chase between Mark McGwire and the Chicago Cubs' Sammy Sosa was credited with bringing millions of fans back to baseball after the players' strike of 1994 drove many away.

Cardinals general manager Walt Jocketty acquired McGwire in a trade with the Oakland Athletics in July 1997. It was a risky move for the club, who surrendered three prospects to Oakland and had no guarantee their new slugger, an impending free agent, would re-sign with the team. Finding a National League strike zone that favored low-ball hitters like himself, and a fan base that traditionally went out of its way to welcome new players, a quickly comfortable McGwire hit 24 home runs during his 51 games in St. Louis. Embracing his new team and city, Big Mac agreed to a new contract before the 1997 season ended and seemed primed for another big year.

McGwire set the pace in 1998, launching 27 home runs by the end of May. Sosa, sitting on just 13 dingers, exploded for 20 in June — still a record for any calendar month — and the race was on. With the Cubs visiting Busch Stadium on September 8, McGwire passed Roger Maris' all-time record of 61 home runs, lining a shot over the left field wall as Sosa watched. It was his shortest homer of the season, measuring 341 feet. Slammin' Sammy drove his 62nd home run five days later and the sluggers traded blows until September 25, when Sosa took a brief lead with his 66th homer. McGwire tied him just minutes later and pulled away with four long balls in his final two games to finish with 70.

Like McGwire, Maris — a former Redbird — was driven by competition when he hit his 61 long balls in 1961, jockeying with New York Yankees teammate Mickey Mantle to match Babe Ruth's total of 60 in 1927. Maris' feat generated debate as Ruth's teams played 154-game seasons and Maris hit his shot in the Yankees' 161st game. Noting the anomaly, Commissioner Ford Frick placed an asterisk in the record book next to Maris' total. McGwire's accomplishment would eventually prove controversial as well, when revelations about steroid use cast a shadow over the 1998 season and an entire era of baseball.

McGwire retired in 2001. He returned to the Cardinals as their hitting coach in 2010, but not before addressing the issue of performance-enhancing supplements. "It's time for me to talk about the past and to confirm what people have suspected. I used steroids during my playing career and I apologize... During the mid-'90s, I went on the disabled list and experienced a lot of injuries... I thought they would help me heal and prevent injuries, too... I wish I had never touched steroids. It was a mistake. I truly apologize. Looking back, I wish I had never played during the steroids era."

"I think it puts baseball back on the map as a sport. It's America's pastime, and just look at everyone coming out to the ballpark. It has been an exciting year." – Mark McGwire

The first home run ball from Mark McGwire's 1998 campaign, hit February 28 in spring training; home plate from his 70th home run in 1998; game-worn cleats from 1999; one of his locker name plates from the era; and two souvenir buttons from the home run race.

MCGWIRE 25

62

1st ROGER DEAN
STADIUM H.R.
2·28·98

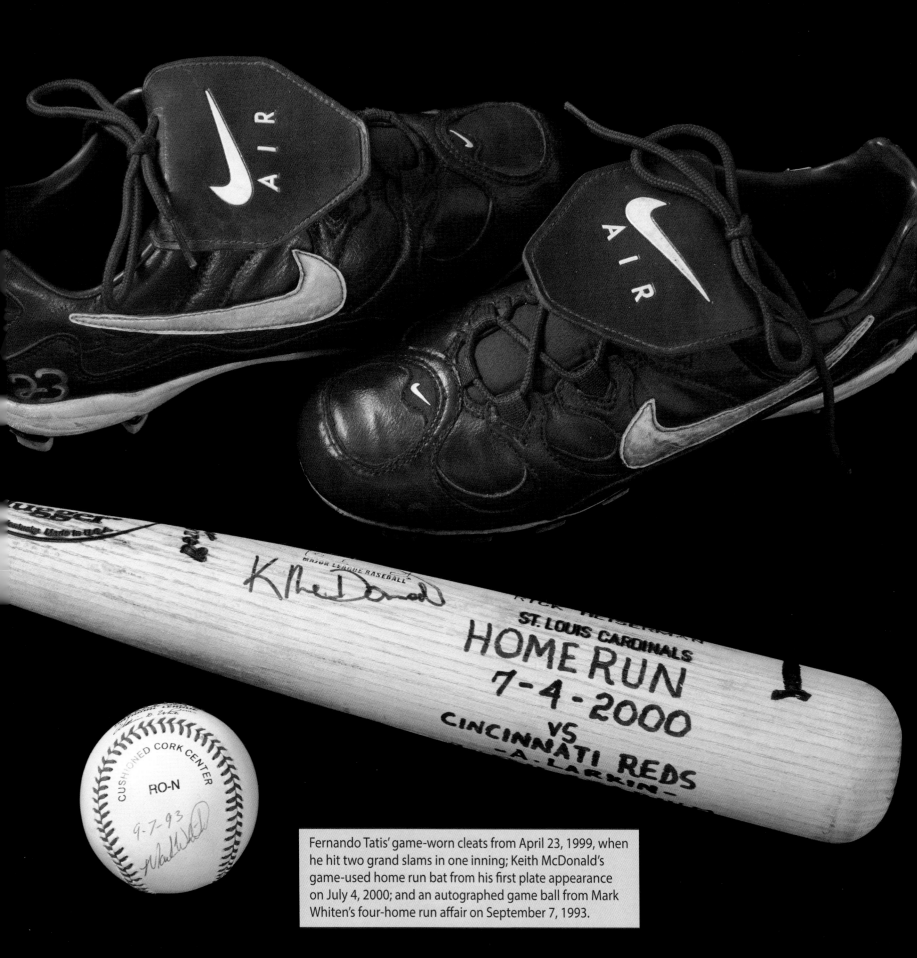

Fernando Tatis' game-worn cleats from April 23, 1999, when he hit two grand slams in one inning; Keith McDonald's game-used home run bat from his first plate appearance on July 4, 2000; and an autographed game ball from Mark Whiten's four-home run affair on September 7, 1993.

Improbable Long Balls

All home runs are exceptional. After all, how many feats in sports *require* a victory lap? But some are more extraordinary, or at least unusual, than others. For example, several Redbirds have hit three longballs in a game — but only one has hit four. Thirteen major leaguers have pounded two grand slams in a single contest — but only one, a Cardinal, hit two — *in the same inning*. And eight Cardinals have slammed long balls in their first Major League at-bats — but one player repeated the feat in his second plate appearance.

Hard-Hittin' Mark Whiten had done little in the majors to deserve the nickname given to him by a former coach but he earned it while playing for St. Louis. Acquired by the Cardinals in 1993, he hit 25 home runs for the club that season with 99 runs batted in. A significant chunk of that production came during the second game of a doubleheader at Cincinnati's Riverfront Stadium on September 7. Whiten hit four home runs, becoming only the 12th player in major league history at the time with four wallops in a single game. He also tied the one-game record of 12 runs batted in, which was set by another Redbird, Jim Bottomley, in 1924.

Whiten's exploits were rare, but what happened April 23, 1999, in a game at Dodger Stadium was practically unthinkable. After driving a grand slam in the third inning, Cardinals third baseman Fernando Tatis stepped to the plate with the bases loaded again — in the same inning, facing the same pitcher — and deposited a ball over the left field fence for a second grand slam. It marked the first time in the 100-plus year history of Major League Baseball that a player hit two grand slams in one inning.

Tatis was fortunate to single in his first big league at-bat, but his career start was not nearly as auspicious as that of Keith McDonald. Matching a feat accomplished by only one player ever — Bob Neiman of the 1951 St. Louis Browns — McDonald homered in his first two at-bats. The initial drive came July 4, 2000, in a pinch-hit appearance; the second two days later. McDonald homered again in his seventh at-bat. It was his third and final hit in the majors.

St. Louis Cardinals Who Homered In Their First Major League At-Bats

Player	Date	Opponent	Player	Date	Opponent
Eddie Morgan	April 14, 1936	Chicago	Gene Stechshulte	April 17, 2001	Arizona
Wally Moon	April 13, 1954	Chicago	Hector Luna	April 8, 2004	Milwaukee
Keith McDonald	July 4, 2000	Cincinnati	Adam Wainwright	May 24, 2006	At San Francisco
Chris Richard	July 17, 2000	At Minnesota	Mark Worrell	June 5, 2008	At Washington D.C.

"I can't believe it happened. I did not expect to hit another one. I've never been a home run hitter. I just try to meet the ball."
– Fernando Tatis on his two-grand slam inning

A simulated baseball game album featuring Jack Buck; an autographed copy of Buck's poem "For America" that he read September 17, 2001; and a KMOX-branded Newsette portable transistor radio.

The Sporting News

THE GREATEST BASEBALL GAME NEVER PLAYED

"THE MYTHICAL CHAMPIONSHIP OF THE UNIVERSE!"

AN LEAGUERS

RS
- zuto, ss (R)
- , cf (L)
- iams, lf (L)
- uth, rf (L)
- nrig, 1b (L)
- rew, 2b (L)
- erra, c (R)
- Robinson, 3b (R)
- Ford, p (L)

SERVES
- Maggio, of (R)
- eaker, of (L)
- Mantle, of (S)
- Jackson, of (L)
- astrzemski, of (L)
- e Foxx, 1b (R)
- ge Sisler, 1b (R)
- Collins, 2b (L)
- ie Gehringer, 2b (L)
- ge Brett, 3b (L)
- Cronin, ss (R)
- Aparicio, ss (R)
- key Cochrane, c (L)
- Dickey, c (L)
- Feller, p (R)
- y Grove, p (L)
- ter Johnson, p (R)
- Young, p (R)
- Palmer, p (R)
- lie Fingers, p (R)
- ylord Perry, p (R)
- sey Stengel, Manager

NATIONAL LEAGUERS

STARTERS
- Pete Rose, 1b (S)
- Mike Schmidt, 3b (R)
- Stan Musial, rf (L)
- Hank Aaron, cf (R)
- Willie Mays, cf (R)
- Rogers Hornsby, 2b (R)
- Honus Wagner, ss (R)
- Roy Campanella, c (R)
- Sandy Koufax, p (L)

N.L. RESERVES
- Mel Ott, of (L)
- Roberto Clemente, of (R)
- Lou Brock, of (L)
- Frank Robinson, of (R)
- Bill Terry, 1b (L)
- John Mize, 1b (L)
- Frank Frisch, 2b (S)
- Jackie Robinson, 2b (R)
- Pie Traynor, 3b (R)
- Eddie Mathews, 3b (L)
- Ernie Banks, ss-1b (R)
- Pee Wee Reese, ss (R)
- Gabby Hartnett, c (R)
- John Bench, c (R)
- Grover Alexander, p (R)
- Warren Spahn, p (L)
- Bob Gibson, p (R)
- Carl Hubbell, p (L)
- Christy Mathewson, p (R)
- Tom Seaver, p (R)
- Steve Carlton, p (L)
- John McGraw, Manager

Hall of Fame broadcasters Lindsey Nelson and Jack Buck create "The Greatest Baseball Game Never Played" for The BFV&L Sports Network.

Highlights of the worldwide broadcast of "The Greatest Baseball Game Never Played" produced by BFV&L Promotions.

NEWSETTE

KMOX

THE BASEBALL STATION

9-11-01

Since this nation was founded... under God
More than 200 years ago,

We have been the bastion of freedom...

The light that keeps the free world aglow.

We do not covet the possessions of others,
We are blessed with the bounty we share.

We have rushed to help other nations...
Anything...anytime...anywhere

War is just not our nature. We won't start,
But we will end the fight.

If we are involved, we shall be resolved to
Protect what we know is right.

We've been challenged by a cowardly foe
Who strikes and then hides from our view.

With one voice we say "there's no choice today."
There is only one thing to do.

Everyone is saying... the same thing... and praying
That we end these senseless moments we are living.

As our fathers did before, we shall win
This unwanted war.

And our children will enjoy the future,
We'll be giving.

Written by Jack Buck on September 14, 2001

Jack Buck

Jack Buck

He walked to the microphone on the Busch Stadium warning track, escorted by tempered applause, and said, "I would like to read a poem which I have written for this occasion." Age and illness had taken their toll, yet his trademark gravelly voice rang strong through the patriotic music while somber fans listened intently.

It was September 17, 2001, the first night of Major League Baseball following the terrorist attacks that shook America six days earlier. The Cardinals — and, in some sense, the entire baseball community — were looking to Jack Buck for comfort, and to validate a return to the field was appropriate. In one of his final public appearances, Buck did what he had done so many times before: He brought the community together. This time it was by reciting an original poem about the American spirit.

Buck began broadcasting Cardinals games in 1954 alongside Harry Caray, forming what many consider the greatest broadcasting duo in the history of the sport. One year later, the Cardinals and local AM station KMOX entered into an exclusive arrangement that would strengthen both institutions dramatically. KMOX owned a 50,000-watt, clear-channel signal for national defense purposes, which meant when other AM stations had to dial back their power after dark, the "mighty MOX" signal stayed strong so citizens could be informed in the event of an attack or disaster. As a result, when conditions were favorable, the voices of Buck and Caray could reach fans in 44 states.

Caray was dismissed from the club in 1969, allowing Buck to move into the primary play-by-play role he would command for more than three decades. During most of those years, he shared the booth with former Cardinals third baseman Mike Shannon. Some of Buck's most memorable calls include Bob Gibson's no-hitter in 1971; Lou Brock's 105th stolen base in 1974; Ozzie Smith's "Go crazy!" home run in Game 5 of the 1985 National League Championship Series; and Mark McGwire's 61st home run in 1998. At the end of every Cardinals victory, Buck offered his trademark phrase, "That's a winner!"

Buck's career extended far beyond Cardinals baseball. He called both baseball and football games nationally for many years on CBS Radio, including a record 17 Super Bowls. His work earned him the highest broadcasting honors from both the National Baseball Hall of Fame and the Professional Football Hall of Fame. The versatile broadcaster even had stints announcing basketball and hockey.

Some 10,000 fans attended his memorial service at Busch Stadium after his passing in 2002, an indication of his status as the most beloved Redbird to never wear a uniform. In fact, he is the only non-playing personality in Cardinals history, other than former owner Gussie Busch, to be honored with a retired number — or more fittingly, a microphone — and a bronze bust at the ballpark.

"After all of these years, I realize my energy comes from the people at the other end." – Jack Buck

Errorless Innings Streak

Whether they're tracking pitch counts, counting the outs until the end of a game or calculating magic numbers in their heads, fans are living proof that baseball is a numbers game. Spectators and franchises alike invest tremendous time and resources following figures, and few are more vigilant than the Redbird faithful. But in the early 2000s, a remarkable streak was taking place at home plate for almost two years, and all but the most ardent observers were unaware.

The Cardinals have long prided themselves in having strong catchers to direct the defense and guide pitchers. Some of the greatest backstops in the game played here, including Roger Bresnahan, Bob O'Farrell, Walker Cooper, Tim McCarver, Ted Simmons, Darrell Porter, Yadier Molina — and Mike Matheny. General Manager Walt Jocketty acquired Matheny in December 1999 and put him in a Cardinals uniform primarily for his defense.

Matheny helped lead the team to the 2000 National League Championship Series during his first year in St. Louis, launching an era of playoff baseball unlike any other in club history. He also won his first of three Rawlings Gold Glove Awards as a Cardinal. But on the last Friday of the regular season, he cut his right ring finger unwrapping a birthday gift — which he didn't realize was a hunting knife until it was too late — and missed the postseason.

The finger recovered, never affecting Matheny's ability to cut down would-be base stealers. He rarely made errors, accumulating just four in both 2001 and 2002. The miscue he made August 1, 2002, though — in a 4-0 shutout loss to the Florida Marlins — would be his last for a long while. In fact, it took 252 games and more than two years before Matheny made another. At the time, it was the longest errorless streak for a catcher in major league history, and it remains a National League record. Along the way, Matheny established another mark for catchers, recording 1,565 chances without an error.

Over the course of his streak, Matheny primarily used one mitt, which now rests in the collection of the Cardinals Museum. Gloves are arguably the most personal piece of equipment baseball players use, and accordingly, players are very protective of them. Matheny donated this mitt (opposite page) only after he had broken in another gamer and had cycled this one out of his rotation. It features a customization where part of the leather was cut out of the first finger area and a piece of quarter-inch thick foam was inserted to provide extra protection in the palm.

After retiring as a player, Matheny returned to manage the Cardinals in 2012 following Tony La Russa's departure. The former backstop is the first skipper in baseball history to lead his team to the playoffs in his first four seasons at the helm.

"I know I haven't put up huge numbers offensively, but I also know what my purpose is on this team—it's behind the plate, and I put a whole lot more pressure and expectations on myself back there." – Mike Matheny

Mike Matheny's game-worn mitt, used for the majority of his National League-record 252-game errorless streak which lasted from August 2, 2002, through August 1, 2004.

Five Home Runs in Five Games

Few players possess the tools that Jim Edmonds displayed on a regular basis in St. Louis. Gifted with a smooth, left-handed power stroke, a strong throwing arm and a knack for tracking down balls into the deepest parts of the outfield, "Jimmy Ballgame" consistently brought fans to their feet.

Edmonds' finest season came in 2004, and while fans remember the critical impact he made with his bat and glove in the playoffs, his productive peak actually occurred in July when he was named the National League's Player of the Month. During that period, Edmonds batted .381 with 32 hits, 27 runs, 13 walks, 13 home runs and 27 runs batted in, adding seven doubles and one triple for good measure. Between July 6 and July 11, he was especially hot, hitting five home runs in five consecutive games. The feat tied a franchise mark set by Jim Bottomley in 1929 and matched by Ripper Collins in 1935. Albert Pujols would join the exclusive club in 2007.

After Edmonds tied the mark, the Museum's staff reached out to him to see if he might donate his now-historic lumber to the team's collection. When there was no immediate response, one of the club's locker room attendants intervened to help clear up any possible confusion. However, Edmonds chose to hold on to his bat — not out of sentiment, but because he genuinely liked hitting with it.

A few weeks following the initial request, and soon after he had been announced as the Player of the Month, a club vice president stopped by the Museum offices with a sanitary sock containing Edmonds' bat. It turns out Edmonds remembered and appreciated the request, but didn't want to give up his Louisville Slugger until he was done using it. The bat was such a favorite that the silver foil-stamping on the barrel, where his name was branded, had completely worn off. There also was a small handle crack underneath the spiral tape job, the condition that forced the bat's retirement.

In an unusual move for the Museum, because the primary markings had disappeared, the staff asked Edmonds to sign and inscribe the piece (opposite page) so that visitors could better appreciate the relic.

Jim Edmonds would enjoy two of the biggest moments of his career during the 2004 postseason with a walk-off home run in Game 6 of the National League Championship Series, followed by a dramatic, game-saving catch in Game 7. But for five games that July, there wasn't a more explosive player on the planet than the Redbirds' sweet-swinging center fielder.

"I was just looking for a ball to get a good swing at. I wasn't trying to go deep. I was trying to hit the ball hard."

– Jim Edmonds, following his home run in Game 6 of the 2004 National League Championship Series

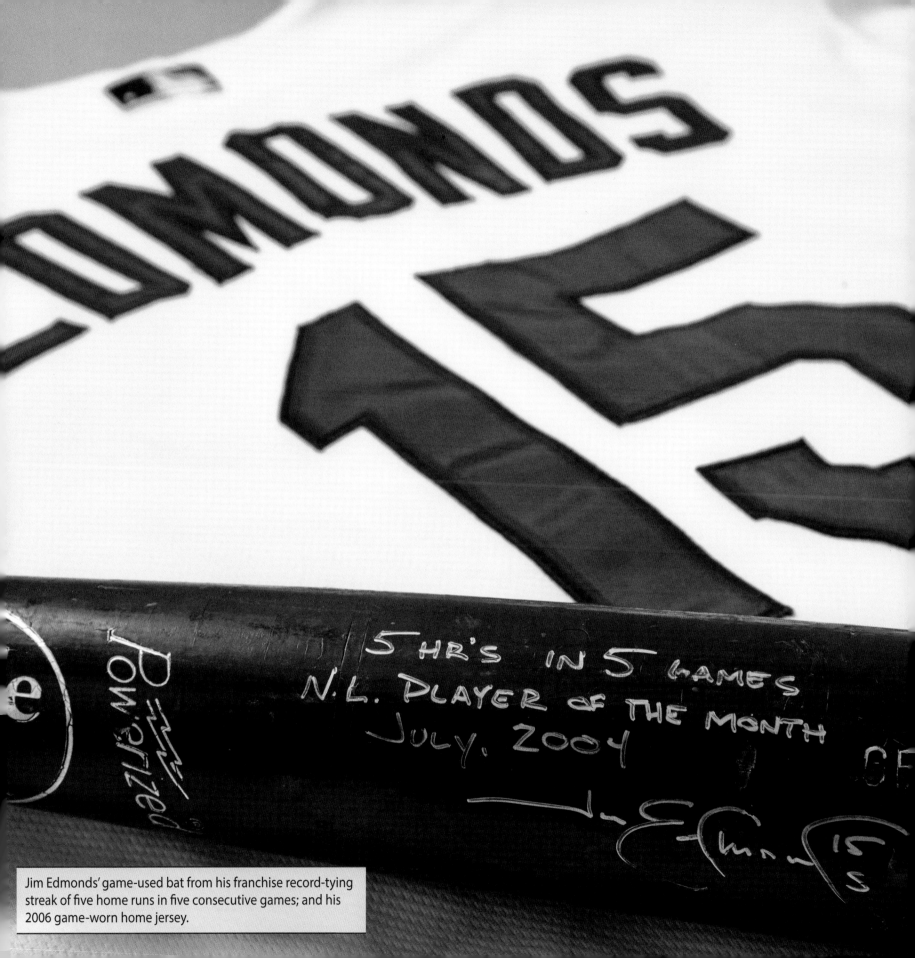

EDMONDS

15

5 HR's IN 5 GAMES
N.L. PLAYER OF THE MONTH
JULY, 2004

Jim Edmonds' game-used bat from his franchise record-tying
streak of five home runs in five consecutive games; and his
2006 game-worn home jersey.

Few pieces of equipment have more personal significance than a player's bat. The Museum maintains more than 400 player bats, with the heaviest weighing 43 ounces and the longest measuring 36 inches.

Hitting for the Cycle

Players come to the ballpark every day hoping to help their teams win by contributing a couple of hits, maybe three if they're really locked in. On rare occasions, though, a batter not only puts together a four-hit night, but does so in the most diverse way possible, stroking a single, double, triple and home run. It's called "hitting for the cycle," and it's happened just 16 times in club history.

The first player in franchise history to hit for the cycle was Cliff Heathcote, a rookie outfielder who needed nine plate appearances to achieve the feat. His contribution was wasted, though, as the Cardinals and Philadelphia Phillies ended their 19-inning affair tied 8-8. Interestingly, the next three Redbirds to record a cycle also did so against Philadelphia pitching.

Joe Medwick notched a cycle at Cincinnati just two seasons before his historic National League Triple Crown campaign, and Stan Musial recorded his at Brooklyn in 1949. "My adrenaline was always flowing in Ebbets Field," Musial once said, and it showed in his performance. He hit .522 in Brooklyn during 1948 and

1949, causing some frustrated fans to remark, "Here comes that man again," whenever he strolled toward the plate. A sportswriter picked up on the buzz, and that's how Musial became "Stan the Man."

Ken Boyer holds the distinction of being the only Cardinals player to hit for the cycle twice, doing so in 1960 and again in 1964. The second time he accomplished it, Boyer became the first Redbird to hit for a "natural cycle," collecting a single, double, triple and home run in succession. John Mabry matched Boyer's feat in 1996.

Lou Brock's combination of speed and power made him an ideal candidate to hit for the cycle, but he completed just one, in 1975. Conversely, the slow-footed Joe Torre seemed like one of the least likely to do it, but he accomplished the feat in 1973. His triple was one of just two he hit that season. The last player to hit for the cycle at Busch Stadium II was Mark Grudzielanek, who did so in an early-season day game vs. Milwaukee in 2005. His bat from that day is part of the Museum collection (opposite page).

St. Louis Cardinals Who Hit for the Cycle

Player	Date	Opponent	Player	Date	Opponent	Player	Date	Opponent
Cliff Heathcote	June 13, 1918	At Philadelphia	Stan Musial	July 24, 1949	At Brooklyn	Willie McGee	June 23, 1984	At Chicago
Jim Bottomley	July 15, 1927	At Philadelphia	Bill White	Aug. 14, 1960	At Pittsburgh	Ray Lankford	Sept. 15, 1991	New York
Chick Hafey	Aug. 21, 1930	Philadelphia	Ken Boyer	Sept. 14, 1961	Chicago	John Mabry	May 18, 1996	At Colorado
Pepper Martin	May 25, 1933	At Philadelphia	Ken Boyer	June 16, 1964	At Houston	Mark Grudzielanek	April 27, 2005	Milwaukee
Joe Medwick	June 29, 1935	At Cincinnati	Joe Torre	June 27, 1973	At Pittsburgh			
Johnny Mize	July 13, 1940	New York	Lou Brock	May 27, 1975	San Diego			

"I was just trying to come up there and have the same approach that I did the previous at-bats and try to hit the ball hard. I stayed back and it worked out. What do you say? It doesn't happen too often. It just was one of those days."
– Mark Grudzielanek after he hit for the cycle

HR, RBI	ST. LOUIS	6
75, 0, 0	22 Eckstein	9
333, 1, 1	33 Walker	3
.333, 0, 0	5 Pujols	5
.222, 0, 0	27 Rolen	8
.200, 1, 4	15 Edmonds	4
.143, 0, 0	12 Grudzielanek	7
.333, 2, 3	16 Sanders	2
.000, 0, 0	41 Molina	1
.000, 0, 0	30 Mulder	

Mark Grudzielanek's game-used bat from April 27, 2005, when he became the last player to hit for the cycle at Busch Stadium II.

BIG STICK
M. GRUDZIELANEK
— PRO —

99 Taguchi	52 Reyes	15 Edmonds, Jim
	56 King	ders, Reggie
		OF
		OF
		COA
		27 Rolen, Scott
		29 Carpenter, Chri
		30 Mulder, Mark
		33 Walker, Larry
		Flores, Rand

Albert Pujols

In the 13th round of the 1999 Major League Baseball First-Year Player Draft, the Cardinals selected Jose Alberto Pujols, a shortstop from Maple Woods Community College. Nobody could possibly foresee that this player — ignored by every team during the first 401 picks — would begin rewriting the big-league record book within a couple of years.

The Dominican Republic native's family moved to Independence, Missouri, by way of New York City, when Pujols was 16 years old. He had demonstrated an adeptness for hitting at a young age, and pursued both baseball and school work with passion. After graduating high school a semester early in December 1998, Pujols enrolled at Maple Woods Community College. That spring he batted .421 and drilled 22 home runs, but scouts were skeptical, citing Pujols' physical build and lack of a "natural" defensive position.

Pujols was disappointed with his draft spot, but decided to make the most of it. In 2000, his only year in the minors, he rapidly progressed through three levels, hitting a combined .314 with 19 home runs, 41 doubles, 74 runs and 96 runs batted in. Named the Class-A Midwest League's Most Valuable Player, Pujols was sent to Triple-A Memphis to finish the season to help the club's postseason chances. His 13th-inning, pennant-winning home run capped a stellar performance that earned him the postseason Most Valuable Player Award.

He made the Cardinals' roster out of spring training in 2001 and never looked back. During his 11-year tenure in St. Louis, Pujols averaged 40 home runs, 121 runs batted in, 117 runs scored and 41 doubles per season. He became the only player in Major League history to hit .300 with at least 30 home runs and 100 runs batted in during each of his first 10 seasons.

Pujols won the National League's Most Valuable Player Award on three occasions and finished in the top five every season in St. Louis except one. That one "off" year offers perspective on just how good Pujols was; he finished ninth in MVP balloting after hitting .327 with 32 home runs and 103 runs batted in.

Albert provided Cardinals fans many memorable moments in his career, including his three-home run performance in Game 3 of the 2011 World Series; his double off Roger Clemens in Game 7 of the 2004 National League Championship Series; and his five-for-five, three-homer day against the Chicago Cubs at Wrigley Field in 2004. His most memorable shot may have occurred in the 2005 National League Championship Series when he hit the "Minute Maid Miracle," a game-winning long ball that let the air out of Houston's ballpark and brought the series back to Busch  Stadium for one final game. Fittingly, Pujols homered in that closing contest — the last by a Redbird in that park — and smashed the first Cardinals home run at the club's new ballpark in 2006.

> *"He's a perfect player. In all categories of the game — hitting, running, defense, cheerleading, being a mentor — you see Hall of Fame greatness."*
> – Tony La Russa, Cardinals manager

Albert Pujols' 2008 home jersey, worn during his second
National League Most Valuable Player Award campaign;
his 2006 game-worn batting helmet; and an autographed
game-used bat from his rookie season.

Yadi and Waino

It was a game for the ages. With the season on the line and a World Series berth at stake, a pair of Redbird phenoms put their stamp on the contest and made an indelible mark on Cardinals history.

Game 7 of the 2006 National League Championship Series between St. Louis and New York had turned into an unexpected pitchers duel between the Mets' Oliver Perez and the Cards' Jeff Suppan. The teams traded single runs through two innings, followed by a chain of goose eggs. The game took a dramatic turn in the top of the sixth, when Scott Rolen drove a ball deep to left field. Mets left fielder Endy Chavez raced back and made an incredible, home run-robbing catch, then threw back to the infield to double off a stunned Jim Edmonds to end the inning.

The Mets rode the momentum into the bottom half of the inning and loaded the bases with one out. "In my mind, I was going to stay away from the curveball in this situation," Suppan says. "I had bases loaded, and I had been in the dirt with the curveball before. And Yadi really wanted to go with the curveball. So I was like, this is it, this is the pitch. I struck him out with one." The Cardinals escaped the jam to keep the score tied.

In the top of the ninth, Molina pounded a dramatic, two-run shot to left, giving the Redbirds a 3-1 lead. "I didn't know right away, but I hit it pretty good," said Yadi. But the Mets loaded the bases in the bottom of the frame as Cardinals-killer Carlos Beltran stepped into the batter's box. "Yadi comes out to the mound, just so we know how we're going to face him. We decided we're going to start him with a fastball away, sinker away," Wainwright explains. "I liked it — let's attack him, let's not be scared of him."

On his way back to the plate, though, Molina had a change of heart. "He points to his chest and says, 'Trust me here.' Yadi has this sign like, 'I'm onto something here, just throw whatever I put down.' He puts down a change-up," Wainwright says. "I hadn't thrown a change-up in probably a month. I threw it right down Broadway, right down the middle. I felt like I had him after that."

Molina then called for a curveball, which Beltran fouled off for strike two. "I said to myself, 'All right, I'm gonna throw the nastiest curveball I have ever thrown. If he hits it, I'll tip my cap, but if not we're going to the Series," Wainwright recalls. "I reached back, and I threw the best curveball I've ever thrown." Beltran froze. Strike three. The Cardinals were 2006 National League champions.

"Molina hits a home run. You think, 'Son of a gun, we're three outs away from being the champions!' And then your heart starts going boom-boom-boom-boom and it's an easy call— here comes Wainwright and then it became just like the movies." – Tony La Russa, Cardinals manager

Yadier Molina's bat from his ninth-inning, pennant-winning home run in Game 7 of the 2006 National League Championship Series; and Adam Wainwright's game-worn cleats from the 2006 campaign.

David Eckstein's game-worn road jersey; Adam Wainwright's game-worn home jersey; a special edition Wheaties® box featuring Chris Carpenter; a Champagne bottle from the World Series clubhouse celebration; the official lineup card from the clinching game; a World Series-issued professional model Jim Edmonds bat; a team-signed ball from the championship club; and the 2006 Commissioner's Trophy.

2006 World Series

The excitement of moving into a new stadium in 2006 could barely mask the frustration of back-to-back 100-win seasons in 2004 and 2005 that each ended without a World Series title. But the Cardinals faithful who convened at baseball's newest cathedral would ultimately be rewarded with one of the most unusual championship runs ever made by the team.

2006 World Series press pin

A string of nagging injuries, especially to regulars Jim Edmonds and David Eckstein late in the year, created a harrowing roller coaster ride through the regular season. The club built a 5.5-game division lead by mid-June, only to lose it after a 1-10 slump. Another 5.5-game lead nearly evaporated in July due to a second eight-game losing streak. The club bounced back, creating a seven-game cushion by September 20, only to drop seven straight. In spite of a 41-52 record down the stretch, the team held on to win the division.

To nobody's surprise, the Cardinals entered the postseason as long shots. That's when something happened that fans had waited for all year — everyone got healthy at the same time. A Division Series win against the San Diego Padres gave the club a boost of confidence before facing the New York Mets in the National League Championship Series. The New Yorkers pushed St. Louis to the brink, but the Redbirds prevailed in dramatic fashion.

The Detroit Tigers, who had swept their way to a pennant in the American League Championship Series, were heavy favorites in the Fall Classic. One national publication sarcastically predicted they'd sweep the Cardinals in three games. The hype didn't affect rookie Anthony Reyes, who retired 17 consecutive batters and outdueled American League Rookie of the Year Justin Verlander for the win in Game 1. Staff ace Chris Carpenter tossed eight scoreless innings in Game 3, and Eckstein collected four hits in Game 4, including two doubles, to position the Redbirds within one victory of a ring.

Midyear pitching acquisition Jeff Weaver, who had a 5.18 earned-run average in 15 Redbird starts entering the postseason, bounced back from a tough-luck loss in Game 2 to tame the Tigers through eight innings in Game 5. Adam Wainwright closed out the game and the Series, which turned out to be one of the most error-prone matchups ever. Of the Cardinals' 22 runs, only 14 were earned, with several resulting from miscues by Tigers pitchers. The Cardinals became the first team since the 1912 Boston Red Sox to capture a Fall Classic at home in the first year of their new ballpark.

2006 Cardinals World Series ring

"No one believed in us, but we believed in ourselves." – David Eckstein, 2006 World Series MVP

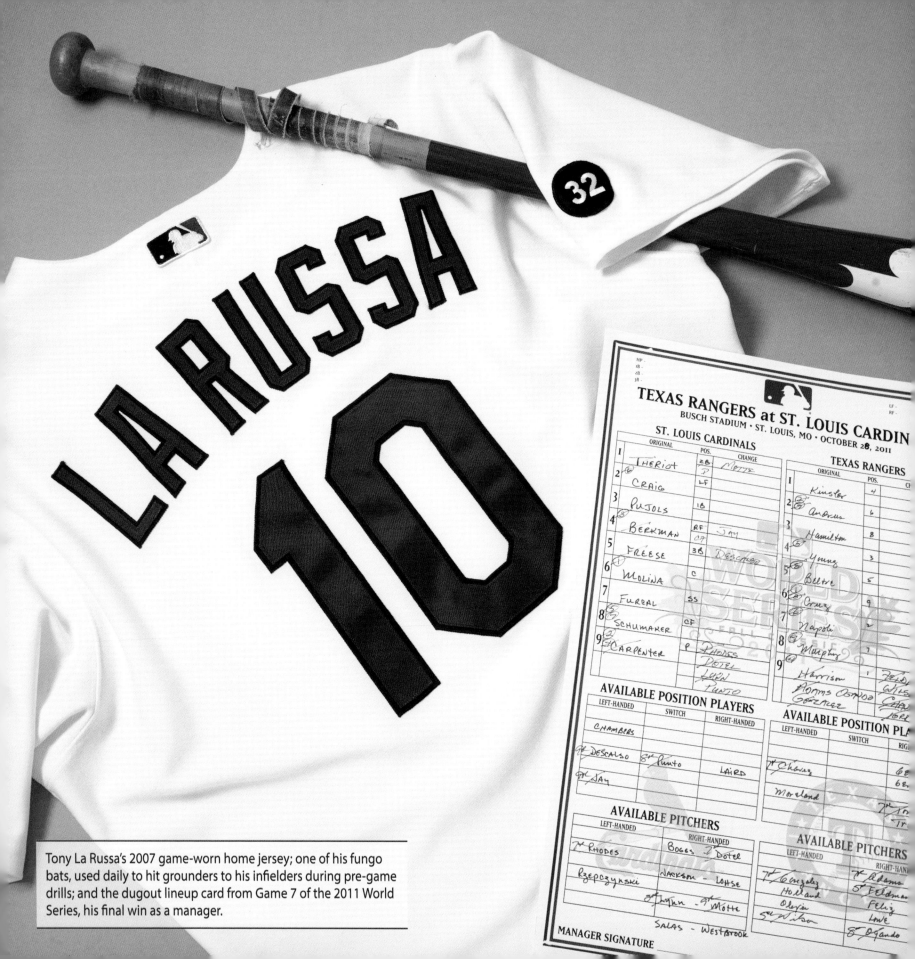

Tony La Russa's 2007 game-worn home jersey; one of his fungo bats, used daily to hit grounders to his infielders during pre-game drills; and the dugout lineup card from Game 7 of the 2011 World Series, his final win as a manager.

Tony La Russa

This forward-thinking manager was often ridiculed by traditionalists because of his aggressive and sometimes unorthodox pursuit of winning. Yet years later, his innovations have altered the game and made him a dugout legend.

A native of Tampa, Florida, Tony La Russa made it to the majors as a middle infielder, playing parts of six seasons with three clubs. When his career as a player-coach in the minors ended, legendary Cardinals instructor George Kissell suggested he consider managing. La Russa took the advice to heart and found a Double-A vacancy the following season. Within two years, he was leading the Chicago White Sox, with whom he won a division title in 1983. La Russa was fired three years later, but landed a new job as manager of the Oakland Athletics before the season ended. He led the A's to three consecutive World Series appearances from 1988-90.

After the 1995 season, La Russa was wooed to St. Louis, a hiring that was endorsed by the new ownership group that took charge in 1996. He selected uniform number 10 to serve as a daily reminder that his objective was to bring a 10th world championship to the Cardinals franchise. La Russa was immediately successful; his club improved by 21 games from the prior year, qualified for postseason play for the first time since 1987, and came within one game of the World Series.

Under La Russa's leadership, the Cardinals embarked upon an era of postseason appearances unmatched in the history of the franchise. Throughout his 16-year tenure, the intense competitor led nine teams into the playoffs, winning a National League pennant in 2004 and World Series titles in 2006 and 2011. His 1,408 wins rank first all-time among Cardinals managers, and his 2,728 total victories rank third in Major League Baseball history.

A skilled tactician, La Russa redefined the role of closer and employed bullpen matchups and varying lineups like no manager before him. He enjoyed squeezing out wins using strategies based on meticulous advanced scouting and always seemed to visualize every possible scenario three or four hitters in advance.

Normally serious in the dugout, La Russa couldn't help but crack a few smiles during his final months in charge. Unknown to most, he had already decided to retire at the end of the 2011 season. In a fitting tribute to one of the greatest skippers in baseball history, the Cardinals made an epic run to the postseason, capped off by one of the most memorable World Series ever. When the final out was made, La Russa burst with emotion. He retired a champion, breaking the news of his plans to his team and the public just days after winning the World Series

> "This is what you dream about. There isn't anybody on this team that, as a young kid, you don't think about winning the World Series, and it's always in Game 7. Truly a dream come true. It's hard to really imagine it actually happened."
> – Tony La Russa after the Redbirds' 2011 world championship

2011 World Series

There are more than a million words in the English language, but attempts to find the right ones to describe the Cardinals' 2011 season fall frustratingly short.

With just 32 games remaining on the schedule, St. Louis found itself 10 games back of division-leading Milwaukee and even further behind the Atlanta Braves in the Wild Card chase. But a 23-9 run, combined with Philadelphia's season-ending sweep of Atlanta, vaulted the Cardinals into the playoffs. The Redbirds met the heavily favored, 102-win Phillies in the Division Series, and split the first four games. In the deciding contest — matching aces Chris Carpenter and Roy Halladay — the Cards scored a run in the first and Carpenter made it hold up, tossing a spectacular, three-hit shutout to advance.

That set up a date with the Brewers, who had outlasted St. Louis to win the Central Division by six games. This time, the Cardinals came out on top four games to two — thanks in large part to the club's bullpen. Manager Tony La Russa made 28 pitching changes during the series to help clinch the pennant.

In the Fall Classic, the Cardinals and Texas Rangers split the first two games at Busch Stadium before reconvening in Texas. In Game 3, Albert Pujols put on possibly the greatest offensive show in a World Series, crushing three home runs, five total hits and six runs batted in as the Redbirds cruised, 16-7. Texas rebounded, though, and carried a three-games-to-two Series lead back to St. Louis.

In Game 6, the Rangers held a 7-5 lead in the bottom of the ninth. With two on, two out and down to his last strike, David Freese tripled to tie the game. Texas' Josh Hamilton silenced the crowd in the 10th with a two-run homer, but the Cards answered in the bottom of the inning as Lance Berkman — also down to his final strike — singled in the tying run. An inning later, St. Louis-native Freese crushed a full-count pitch deep into the October night for a Cardinals win. At home plate, the hero's jersey was "shredded" in the chaos, a tradition started earlier in the year by utility infielder Nick Punto. Typically, jersey fronts would simply pop open. On this night, though, the wildly exuberant players tore Freese's jersey in two.

Carpenter surrendered two runs in the first inning of Game 7, but he and four relievers held the Rangers in check the rest of the way. Freese's two-run double tied the contest after one frame and Allen Craig's third-inning blast put the Cardinals ahead for good.

2011 World Series press pin

2011 World Series ring

"That game had everything in it. People were crying, people were laughing, people were hugging and people were screaming. It had every emotion possible."
– David Freese, 2011 World Series MVP, describing the Cardinals' 10-9 win in Game 6

A remnant of David Freese's game-worn 2011 World Series jersey, torn in two by excited teammates after his walk-off home run in Game 6; the 2011 Commissioner's Trophy; and one of Lance Berkman's bats from the 2011 postseason.

World Series Obstruction

It was Game 3 of the 2013 World Series. Bottom of the ninth. Score tied. One out. Runners on second and third. The crowd watched anxiously as the ball was hit into a drawn-in infield. The second baseman made a diving stop, jumped to his feet and threw home to cut down the lead runner. Two outs. The catcher then fired to third base in hopes of an inning-ending double play. But the throw went into left field. The runner broke for home. The left fielder grabbed the ball and unleashed a laser toward the catcher, who tagged the sliding runner. It was a bang-bang play. All eyes were on home plate umpire Dana DeMuth. But, instead of ruling out or safe, he... pointed to his colleague at third base?

Most of the 47,000-plus fans in attendance didn't know whether to cheer or prepare for extra innings. Players from both teams began to wander onto the field — the Cardinals, to check on their shaken young base runner, Allen Craig, who clearly had aggravated a nagging foot injury; and the Boston Red Sox, in search of an explanation. As the arbiters convened, a realization began spreading through the stands.

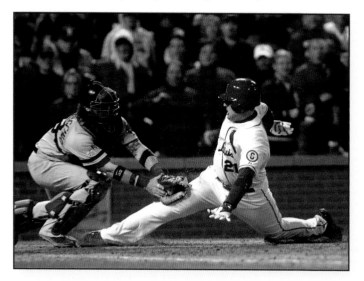

Third-base umpire Jim Joyce had flagged the fielder for obstruction. The run counted. The game was over. The Cardinals had won, 5-4.

The decision acknowledged that the catcher's throw pulled Boston third baseman Will Middlebrooks into the baseline between second and third, and directly into the path of a sliding Craig. As Craig touched the base and popped up, he became tangled with the prone fielder, tripping and falling before making a break for home. Whether it was accidental or an intentional act by Middlebrooks—who kicked his feet into the air — was irrelevant. Craig's ability to make an unobstructed dash toward the plate was prevented by contact. Joyce awarded Craig the base and gave the Cardinals the win. This dirt-stained jersey (opposite page) is the one Craig wore that day during his "obstacle-course" around the bases.

The Cardinals are no strangers to unique Fall Classic endings. Just a day after the aforementioned obstruction call, Redbird second baseman Kolten Wong was picked off first base to end Game 4. Until that point, no Series game in history had ever ended with fielder's obstruction or a pick off. St. Louis also was involved the only time a World Series ended with a runner caught stealing; the victim was Babe Ruth, whose ill-advised baserunning attempt resulted in the franchise's first world championship in 1926. And while David Freese's dramatic 11th-inning home run in Game 6 of the 2011 World Series wasn't the only walk-off long ball in Series history, that game did mark the only time a league champion was down to its final strike twice in an elimination game, only to come back to win.

"That was one of the craziest plays I've been a part of." – Allen Craig

Allen Craig's 2013 home-alternate World Series jersey, worn during Game 3 when an obstruction call awarded him home plate and ended the game.

Matt Holliday's 2015 home jersey, worn when he set the league on-base record to start a season; Kolten Wong's 2014 batting practice jersey; Matt Carpenter's 2012 game-used glove; a game-used ball from Michael Wacha's first major league win; Trevor Rosenthal's 2013 game-worn home playoff cap; and a Carlos Martinez model bat used by his good friend, Oscar Taveras, in 2014.

Collecting Current Artifacts

On May 27, 2015, Matt Holliday stroked a single in the fifth inning against the Arizona Diamondbacks at Busch Stadium. It didn't drive in the lead run or honestly impact the game's outcome in any way. But behind the scenes, a process began to ensure the hit would be remembered by Cardinals fans for generations to come.

Holliday's line drive was no mere single — it established both a franchise record and the National League mark for reaching base in consecutive games to begin a season. The left fielder touched first base safely for the 43rd straight game, a stretch of consistency worthy of a place in the Cardinals Museum.

Following the game, Holliday's jersey was tagged with a hologram by an official representative of Major League Baseball, and the sticker's unique serial number was logged in to the league's authentication database. The process was created in 2001 to provide objective, third-party authentication that guarantees game-used and autographed memorabilia are genuine. This offers peace of mind for fans who buy souvenirs through the Cardinals Authentics Shop and similar outlets, but the arrangement also benefits the club and the Cardinals Museum. In this case, a gracious Holliday chose to give his jersey to the Museum to be archived for posterity.

The slugger's jersey joined more than 22,000 other items of historical significance the club maintains. Considered the largest team collection in professional sports, the Museum's artifacts encompass the history of baseball in St. Louis beyond the Cardinals. The American League Browns, the Negro League Stars, and even some of the short-lived clubs from baseball's early days are also represented in the archives.

Since the current ownership group — led by Bill DeWitt Jr., a passionate baseball historian — purchased the club in 1996, the Museum's holdings have grown dramatically both in size and quality. The variety of items runs the gamut. Game-used jerseys, bats, balls and gloves—along with World Series trophies and rings — are among the featured artifacts. But there also are players' personal items and awards, stadium giveaways and thousands of paper items — from scorecards and photos to scouting reports and stadium blueprints. The collection even includes a violin and a kimono.

The Cardinals Museum is more than a place to gaze at treasures from the past. A variety of interactive exhibits allow fans to hold an authentic game bat used by a Cardinals great; take the microphone to call a famous moment in team history; mark their hometowns on an electronic map of Cardinals Nation; and learn more about players on the active roster. A few steps from the Museum's entrance, guests can also read plaques honoring members of the Cardinals Hall of Fame.

The St. Louis Cardinals Hall of Fame and Museum *is* where tradition meets today.

> *"There are some great pitchers out there, and we've faced a lot of them. To find your way on base in that many games in a row in the National League is pretty good."*
> –Matt Holliday on his record on-base streak

References, Sources and Credits

References

Achorn, Edward. *The Summer of Beer and Whiskey: How Brewers, Barkeeps, Rowdies, Immigrants, and a Wild Pennant Fight Made Baseball America's Game.* New York: Public Affairs, 2013.

Barthel, Thomas. *Pepper Martin: A Baseball Biography.* Jefferson: McFarland, 2003.

Broeg, Bob. *Stan Musial: "The Man's" Own Story.* Garden City: Doubleday & Company, Inc., 1964.

Cash, Jon David. *Before They Were Cardinals: Major League Baseball in Nineteenth-Century St. Louis.* Columbia: University of Missouri Press, 2002.

Cohen, Robert W. *The 50 Greatest Players in St. Louis Cardinals History.* Lanham: The Scarecrow Press, Inc., 2013.

Diagnostic and Statistical Manual of Mental Disorders, 4th Edition, Text Revision. Arlington: American Psychiatric Association, 2000.

Eisenbath, Mike. *The Cardinals Encyclopedia.* Philadelphia: Temple University Press, 1999.

Feldmann, Doug. *St. Louis Cardinals Past & Present.* Minneapolis: MVP Books, 2009.

Golenbock, Peter. *The Spirit of St. Louis: A History of the St. Louis Cardinals and Browns.* New York: HarperCollins, 2000.

Heidenry, John. *The Gashouse Gang.* New York: PublicAffairs, 2007.

Lamb, Scott and Tim Ellsworth. *Pujols: More Than the Game.* Nashville: Thomas Nelson, 2011.

Leach, Matthew. *Game of My Life: St. Louis Cardinals: Memorable Stories of Cardinals Baseball.* New York: Sports Publishing, L.L.C., 2008

Phillips, Thomas D. *Touching All the Bases: Baseball in 101 Fascinating Stories.* Lanham: The Scarecrow Press, Inc., 2012.

Poekel, Charlie. *Babe & The Kid: The Legendary Story of Babe Ruth and Johnny Sylvester.* Charleston: The History Press, 2007.

Rains, Rob. *Albert Pujols: Simply the Best.* Chicago: Triumph Books, 2009.

Wheatley, Tom. The Memoirs of Bing Devine: Stealing Lou Brock and Other Winning Moves by a Master GM. New York: Sports Publishing, L.L.C., 2004.

McCarver, Tim and Phil Pepe. Few and Chosen: Defining Cardinal Greatness Across the Eras. Chicago: Triumph Books, 2003.

Sullivan, Kenneth. *"A Batboy Watches the World's Series,"* in Play the Game: The Book of Sport, edited by Mitchell V. Charnley. New York: Viking Press, Inc., 1931.

Lester, Larry. *Black Baseball's National Show-case: The East-West All-Star Game, 1933-53.* Lincoln: University of Nebraska Press, 2001.

Sources

Baseball-Almanac.com

Baseball-Reference.com

The Boston Globe

Louisville Slugger

MLB.com

National Baseball Hall of Fame and Museum

New York Post

The New York Times

Rawlings Sporting Goods

Retrosimba.com

San Antonio Express-News

Smithsonian Magazine

Society for Amercian Baseball Research (SABR) SABR Baseball Biography Project

Sports Illustrated

St. Louis Cardinals Communications Department

St. Louis Cardinals Gameday Magazine

St. Louis Post-Dispatch

St. Petersburg Times

The Sporting News

Vivaelbirdos.com

The Washington Post

Photo Credits